Contents

Introduction		4

Part 1   **The potential of your organisation's events**

Chapter 1	The role of events in your organisation	8
Chapter 2	The difference between the member service ethos and the commercial ethos	16
Chapter 3	Are events always the right option?	21
Chapter 4	Addressing processes within the organisation	26
Chapter 5	What an excellent events team looks like	32

Part 2   **How to make your events more commercial**

Chapter 6	Nine steps to organising fantastic events	38
Chapter 7	The importance of setting objectives	44
Chapter 8	How to choose the right events	50
Chapter 9	Events marketing strategy	58
Chapter 10	Addressing the processes within the events team	65
Chapter 11	Why you always have to concentrate on costs	72
Chapter 12	How to decide on the right price for your events	78
Chapter 13	When and how to outsource parts of the events process	84

Conclusion		89
Bonus appendix		91
Links to electronic appendix		95

Introduction

The room is packed full of event organisers, most of whom represent membership bodies and trade associations. An events manager from a large membership organisation has the floor. She has just run through her case study covering the changes she's battled against in her organisation to try and streamline her events processes. She's had a hard time that much is obvious from her presentation, but what is more obvious is her steely determination, *"Sometimes I just do things, and ask if they are OK later"* she says. Everyone in the room laughs while admiring her boldness.

Her story continues as she gives details of her team of eight organisers managing around 100 events. Not too bad I think. I wonder if they make any money for the organisation? I raise my hand and the Chairman points in my direction, I take his cue, *"It sounds like you've done a great job, I was wondering if you take into account operating costs for your events department; does it make any profit?"* "We call it surplus, not profit", she answers. I rephrase my question, *"Are you making a contribution to surplus?"* She smiles, "No, we are still running at a loss, but we hope to breakeven soon".

What a shame. A great organiser, full of ideas, experienced and in a very strong position to provide a better service to her members while stopping her team being a drain on the organisation. If only she was supported by senior management in the organisation who just knew that little bit more about an increasingly important part of their business. If she was given an objective to make a positive contribution (a surplus or profit - they are the same thing) while improving her events, I have no doubt she would be able to do it.

At another event for Director Generals and Chief Executives of trade associations, several 'scenarios' are presented and discussed. The scenario planning exercise is there to test how the sector will cope with potentially damaging change. I am shocked to see one particular 'dangerous' scenario presented: it is entitled: "The Trade Association has a strong profit motive."

After the scenario is worked through from the stage, I ask the presenter a question, *"Is trying to generate a profit that bad an idea? I've strengthened trade associations by putting them on a much sounder commercial footing while at the same time improving the overall service to members. Rather than a danger, a commercialisation of parts of your organisation can actually be a saviour."* Suspicious looks all round. I feel like the "profit pariah".

These examples, along with my experience over 10 years working in this sector, were the spark that lit the fire beneath this book. If only I could provide senior managers with a bit more knowledge about events and help event organisers get the most out of their events our sector could function so much better. If the question is how can we deliver more value? The answer is operating more commercially. Some not for profit organisations have a long journey ahead of them to embrace a commercial ethos and in some this idea seems to run contrary to their fundamental beliefs; but operating more commercially only really means watching the pennies and the pounds and who can argue with that as a sensible approach in any organisation? As events plays such a crucial part in many not for profit organisations it is an ideal place to start commercialisation. As I will demonstrate in this book the outcome of a commercial approach tends to be a better service for all, which adds substantially more value to your stakeholders.

This is currently the only book that is designed to help senior professionals in the not for profit sector analyse their approach to organising events. The focus is on providing more for your members/stakeholders pound, or as I've put it: commercialising your events (I will demonstrate that they are the same thing). Even if the events you run are purely not for profit and attendance is free, you will still gain knowledge from every single section of this book.

This book is about delivering quality events, on budget and on time, with many tips on how to control this process. It's about bottom line and it's about delivery. It's not all about profit (like your organisation), it is about providing a service to members or stakeholders who've already paid some money to the organisation and expect a quality product. Finally, it is about making sure you deliver the most cost effective event, allowing much needed resources and finance to be deployed elsewhere, be that to other departments, or straight onto your department's bottom line.

What do we mean by commercialisation in not for profit organisations?

Most organisations in the Government, not for profit and charity sector are public bodies or member driven organisations and are justly regarded as non commercial organisations. They carry out their role in society funded by donation, by the public purse, by individual members or by company subscriptions. They operate 'not for profit' but almost every organisation where possible will try to make some use of its services to generate income, so in some terms, there is a commercial aspect in every not for profit, to paraphrase Wilfred Owen the first world war poet; there is a small piece of your organisation, that will forever be trying to make a profit.

The enterprise/commercial parts of your organisation, especially in membership bodies and trade associations, can be some of the most strongly driven surplus centres in the commercial world. Having such a money driven centre in a not for profit organisations could strike you as a paradox, but it's true. The reason for this is the majority of the staff in the building at not for profit organisations are not there to raise income: these little teams are. This being the case, the commercial part has to be extremely focussed on earning revenue while the other parts of the organisations work on justifying its existence to members/stakeholders by providing valuable services.

In today's uncertain market conditions the stability, and often the survival of some organisations, depends upon their commercial team, with events playing a big part of that commercial income. Without the revenue generated by this team, supporting the other functions of the organisation is terribly difficult. That is a lot of pressure for your commercial team and it's why they need support and understanding from the rest of the organisation.

What you will gain from this book

This book is designed to allow senior managers and leaders within not for profit organisations to gain an understanding and an insight into the true potential of their events. The book is also designed to help event, marketing and commercial managers to move away from the practical and the tactical, allowing them to focus on how their roles should focus on the strategic position events should play in the not for profit sector.

The book is also a practical manual for the organiser. It is structured to allow you to evaluate every process within your events department and give you the confidence to make changes. Every example is practical and has a proven success in various not for profit organisations.

Part 1

The potential of your organisation's events

Chapter 1

The role of events in your organisation

Almost all not for profit organisations will run events for their members or stakeholders. Events offer a tried and tested way to keep your stakeholders up to date with recent regulation; thoughts; discussions and decisions affecting their particular area of interest. Events also offer an excellent vehicle for communications from your organisations. Events can normally deliver messages in a different way to other means that you deploy and can deliver those messages in a cost effective way. Events can, while delivering those messages, even sometimes generate income.

Even without a commercial view events tick a lot of boxes for our organisations so it is understandable why many organisations start with the premise that running an event is always an excellent idea. And in summary here's what we are likely to think. Events are:

1. Easy to measure in terms of their success
2. Very visible
3. An obvious way to demonstrate to your members and stakeholders that you are providing a service for them

For all the reasons above events will continue to play a vital role in the operations of our organisations.

Types of events that you will organise

Events that your organisation will run fall broadly into 4 categories, here are the formats that you should be familiar with:

- **Training events:** small number of attendees, 10-30 delegates, with lengthy preparation and detailed content, usually one speaker, and a relatively high price to attend

- **Seminars and conferences:** anything from 40-1000 delegates and beyond, a lead-in time reflecting the size of the event, several speakers, mid priced events

- **Exhibitions and fairs with 6 to 600 stands:** learning is important but so is the involvement of external companies who are ostensibly there to recruit or sell

- **Dinners, awards or other similar social events:** small gatherings up to gala dinner spectaculars for thousands, mainly there to raise money or profile. There are a myriad of events like this

Anything smaller than these 'events' are normally meetings and seldom need the involvement of the events professional as they are mainly administrative and can be run by secretaries or other roles which have the capacity for 'helping out'.

What your events should do - variety is the key

When we start to look at the commercial role of events it becomes clear that you should be offering your members and stakeholders as wide ranging and diverse selection of events as possible.

In a well run commercial business more events should mean more profit but we also have to consider that the more extensive the choice of events offered the more likely you are to increase your chance of satisfying each member/stakeholder's needs. This choice, if well managed, should allow you to offer a full range of events to your members, and to make sure that you are leaving no stone unturned In your search for commercial income.

How events differ

The duration and timings (half day, full day, evening session) the format (main sessions, discussions, breakouts sessions) the means for delivery (online, face-to-face), the location and the price, should be structured sufficiently different to allow potential attendees to decide how they wish to engage with other members and the wider stakeholder community. Offering a wide choice of events will allow your delegates/guests to decide what the most suitable way is for them to access information and knowledge from your organisation.

Chapter 1 - The role of events in your organisation

A large number of not for profit organisations tend to cover topics once, in one particular way: normally the delegate-paid-for one day annual conference.

Question: Is the one day conference your fallback position for all your events?

Question: Do your conversations around a hot topic normally start with "can we run a one day conference on this topic"?

If the one day conference is the only option you offer to delegates, you may be missing out on attendees who would be interested in the topic but not the format or the delivery. Or maybe the price for a one day event is too high, or the location is not convenient. How can these people engage with you if your offering is always the same?

As you are there to provide a service to all of your members/stakeholders where possible you should be thinking about all of them and considering different styles and a variety of events.

Most of your events are likely to be around sharing/gaining knowledge, and of course, the likely demand for information or knowledge on a particular topic will be finite but you have to look at all the options and offer choice where possible. It is the same for events that are arranged with a social or a networking agenda like dinners and lunches. There will only be so many events like this you can organise but it would be worth looking at changing times, length, duration etc.

Example

The following example printed with permission from the Council of Mortgage Lenders (CML) in 2010 demonstrates how a mixed set of events can be used to make sure that all members have the opportunity to choose how they wish to engage with their trade association on a particular topic.

With an anticipated rise in the likely number of houses being repossessed and the considerable amount of legislation and regulation in this area disseminating information on how to help lenders deal with this area was paramount to the CML.

Chapter 1 - The role of events in your organisation

The Council of Mortgage Lenders commercial offering around mortgage arrears and possessions

Commercial products targeting members who had customers in arrears or with properties in possession: 2010

February
"Arrears and possessions conference", full day, Manchester. £365
Webcasting of the above conference, available next day £365

March
Launch of updated arrears and possessions e-learning course (14 modules) priced £250 per licence
"Arrears and possessions in Scotland conference", full day, Edinburgh. £275

June
"Dealing with properties in possession" half day seminar hosted by asset management companies, member only, London, free to attend

September
"Arrears and possessions conference" full day, London, £365

November
Plenary session at main CML conference

Run four times a year
"Delivering the right debt advice to customers" workshops, full day detailed training £400. Course also delivered in house.

"Helping customers in arrears gain access to benefits" workshops, full day detailed training £400. Course also delivered in house.

As you can see the CML was doing everything it could to offer its members a variety of formats, delivery channels and prices which would allow members to keep up to date with a rapidly changing environment.

Crucially, as we will demonstrate in the following chapter, sitting alongside these events were a host of other services, policy work and resources available to members as part of their membership fee.

Ensuring that mortgage lenders were dealing properly with properties and more importantly with the people involved was an exceptionally important objective for the CML. Events were not the whole answer in delivering messages to members and stakeholders, but they played a crucial role in helping deliver this important organisational goal.

Question: When planning events do you link them to your organisation's goals?

Chapter 1 - The role of events in your organisation

Using events to target non-members and the wider community to subsidise membership fees

One of the most important roles events should play is to generate an income, which if used properly can subsidise membership fees. There can be no better or a more popular way to fund your organisation than earning income from outside your membership. This earning power is an important part of the role that your events can play, however this potential is something that a lot of not for profits have been slow to appreciate. Sure, they can generate a few pounds here and there, but really can they generate enough money from outside our membership to affect the levels of subs?

In a strong commercial events strategy your events should; firstly target your members and then secondly target non-members: be they associate members or a wider community interested in your particular sector.

Proving that events can do more than just generate profit

Heaven forbid your organisation views events simply as a way to deliver some information to members or stakeholders. Events can do so much more. Your objectives for events should go beyond a member service; to address member retention; earn a significant income; generate new members and even affect the policy direction of your organisation.

Events can be great public-facing occasions at which, for example, the industry can start to fight back on a controversial issue. Events can be subtle; they can prove that your industry is interested in a particular topic that perhaps the outside world doesn't think you care about.

Example - The British Bankers' Association Annual Responsible Lending Conference

Around 2003 the banking industry as a whole was reluctant to recognise the term "responsible lending", and the implication, therefore, that some lending had been "irresponsible". However at the banking industry trade body, the British Bankers' Association (BBA), some of the policy team, and an event manager were very keen

Chapter 1 - The role of events in your organisation

to help members address this issue. Some of the larger banks were forward thinking on this issue and were also keen for the industry to recognise the growing levels of over-indebtedness in the UK, caused in part, by some irresponsible lending. But this view was not shared by the whole membership.

The event manager was very keen to run an annual conference looking at these issues and believed most of the membership would be interested in hearing, and perhaps shaping, what the industry was doing. And as a good commercial events manager they were pretty sure that enough people would turn up to make some money for the association.

It was strange at the time for the event manager to be taking an active part in pushing the policy direction of the BBA through an event, but it worked. The event made some money, and shortly after, owing to the positive media coverage, the industry became much more open in recognising the general concerns of "over-indebtedness". The event became an annual conference and ran for seven years.

Principles that should underpin your current events strategy

As described above, harnessing the ideas of the event manager, and running events with a wider recognition of the organisational goals is a principle of good not for profit event management. But there are others too.

The events you run and the reasons for running those events will be totally different from other entities that organise events. The not for profit events world is and has to be different. In order to put your events in the right context we will look at how your events differ from those in the pure commercial events world.

- It's likely that you, a Committee, papers supplied through a 'call of papers' process, or a policy team will decide the topics which need to be covered in an event programme and you don't often dedicate a large resource to finding out if these ideas are backed by a demand

- Your market research is effectively done by your Committee or policy team and the time you spend on external research is fairly low

Chapter 1 - The role of events in your organisation

- Your events are related to a narrow field in pharmaceutical, telecoms, finance, housing, manufacturing, etc.
- The events team is organising events that the rest of your organisation is able to support
- You target volume business. You would rather have more people paying less than a few paying a substantial amount, and so your price is in the middle range for your market
- To a large degree your brand alone sells your events. Your badge or name has a strong association with good content, delivery and trust
- What you do is part of a larger organisation
- Your unique selling point (USP) is built around events being for your members, or on behalf of your stakeholders and an understanding that your objectives, unlike all your competitors, are not entirely driven by profit
- Your events are more than profit making machines and can fulfil other wider organisational objectives

In summary your events are not wholly profit driven and are only a part of the wider role of your organisation.

It is very easy to look at events run by commercial event companies and try to benchmark your events against their events. This is a common approach when not for profit organisations really look to sweat their existing list of events but it is rarely the right approach.

Companies in the commercial events world will mirror every style and every possible event topic you cover, as well as a variety of other formats and use of delivery channels and price. When senior managers in not for profit organisations can look at similar events run by commercial event companies they can point to a higher involvement of sponsors; higher delegate prices and high profile speakers. This justifiably allows them to wonder why their events are different and appear to make less money. There is no doubt that looking at the leading events in your sector can be a good thing but you have to realise what it is about your events that make them different from those run by the commercial sector.

Chapter 1 - The role of events in your organisation

Example

In one membership body their events department was modelled on a successful commercial conference company. From staff job descriptions, to systems and procedures the membership body's event department mirrored a purely commercial events business. The organisation in question would not recognise any of the principles above and it was no surprise to see a poorly functioning and ironically, profitless, events department. What was good for the commercial goose was certainly not good for the not for profit gander: they were running a lot of events but weren't making any money!

In setting up like a commercial events business they were missing out on all of the USP's that our organisations have. A quick review of the principles demonstrated quickly to them that they were following a false God. Embrace the differences.

The list above will hopefully put in context the events you organise and also highlight some key differences with commercial event companies. It will also allow us to look in the next chapter at the events you offer within the context of the other products and services you give to your members and stakeholders. It can also be a good and quick benchmarking process to see if your organisation and the events team are doing anything markedly different from what is best practice in a good commercial event department in a not for profit organisation.

Chapter 2
The difference between the member service ethos and the commercial ethos

A lot of trade associations and membership bodies strive, but struggle to achieve a balance between the "member service" and the "commercial" side of their organisation. In order to stay viable organisations know they have to provide products and services, as part of their membership fee or subscription, and they have to earn extra income from other sources beyond those subscriptions and fees. So where should events sit? Should they be included in the membership fee or as part of that additional income?

Before we look at where events sit within the total offering of your organisation we have to settle on a definition of what we mean by "commercial" and "member service".

What we mean by member service

The member service is a series of products and or services provided to members as part of the fee, or subscription. The organisation does things on behalf of the fee payer or subscriber, like lobbying, or regulating, or defending and representing the industry. It also provides some products like newsletters, policy updates, access to panels, detailed research, help line etc. at no additional charge.

What we mean by commercial

On top of your member service the organisation will also arrange things that the members and other people, such as non members and the wider stakeholder community, can choose to pay for. The organisation will have publications, which cost something to buy, or it may collect information from members and look to sell it. And of course there will be commercial events that are paid for by the delegates. Most if not all trade associations and membership bodies operate like this and the basis of this model is even increasingly being looked at for Government bodies.

The commercial approach

In a commercial events department there is an understanding that the department should have financial targets at its core. You will be amazed by how many events departments, who think they operate commercially, do not have financial targets. An important point is that the financial target doesn't have to be a positive one, it can be a negative one, if that suits the organisation better; a negative target is better than no target at all.

Understanding that an events business focussing on costs and expenditure will deliver a better service to members is the most crucial factor in a department operating or striving to become more commercial. This commerciality can be reflected in the name of the department but it is also understood in the culture within the events team and fundamentally, it has to be shared by the wider culture of the organisation.

This naturally invites you to take a look at your events department and to reflect.

Question: Do you feel that your event department is already commercial?

You can look out for the obvious signs like a financial target and a good cost cutting culture and it's unlikely that you are commercial if either of these cornerstones are missing. It's also unlikely that you have a commercial ethos in your events department if you hear any of the following:

- "can you organise the event very much along the same lines as last year"
- "but it's what people expect"
- "it's what we've always done"
- "the members/guests/delegates aren't telling us that's an issue or a problem so why change?"
- "we are all event experts here!"
- "it's OK, confirm the venue now, we don't want to lose it, I am sure we'll get enough people to come"

Chapter 2 - The difference between the member service ethos and the commercial ethos

If you ever hear these phrases in your events department, or if you ever ask your staff to *"organise an event exactly like last year"*, the correct commercial ethos isn't ingrained in your organisation. These are 'sign post' phrases and if you ever hear them or say them, and you wish to become more commercial your ethos has to change.

Finding a place for your events department in the wider organisation

When your events department sits in its little silo, without commercial targets, or allowed to set its commercial targets, separate from the other departments, it is not working to its full potential. As the generators of a large income for the organisation, and part of the public face of your organisation, it is extremely important - actually it is vital - that your events department understands the overall position of your organisation and your organisational culture.

It is equally important that the organisation knows the role and the objectives of your events department. In too many organisations the little events team is scowled upon as the group of people who "make money out of members", while the rest of the organisation services those members. For a not for profit organisation to thrive, the department generating the profit has to work with every other part of the organisation.

Question: Where does your commercial area sit in your organisation?
Is it on a separate floor? One corner of the room?

In many organisations the member service area is seen as the black sheep of the family and no real effort has been made to integrate it properly into the organisation. It is very rarely near the centre of the building or in the middle of the office floor, or physically at the heart of the organisation.

Trying to find a policy officer who knows the objectives of the events department can be impossible. It is up to senior management, especially if you are starting a process of change, to explain to the wider organisation that:

Chapter 2 - The difference between the member service ethos and the commercial ethos

The department can only make money from members or stakeholders by providing a fantastic service

The service the events team provides adds to the member experience, it doesn't detract from it

Targeting your events at non members and the wider stakeholder community

Another difference between the member service and the commercial department is the targeting of attendees out with your membership. As a wider organisational strategy the widening and opening up of your commercial intellectual property to other individuals and organisations should be a priority. There is no better way of opening up and earning income from your commercial IP than through events.

Income from your commercial events department will subsidise the core services your organisation provides for your members and stakeholders. The core services you offer are covered by subscriptions and the additional services are a choice, for your members to take or not. The chargeable services generate an income that can be reinvested in the core services.

Rather than have your members subsidise themselves, why not focus some of your events at non members and have them subsidise your members? This approach is distinctive in the difference between a commercially focussed events department and a member service ethos led department.

Most not for profit organisations open up their events to non members, but not many focus on non members as a separate income stream and this is where real growth can be made and only fully functioning commercial departments can do this successfully.

Programme content covered at your events will be interesting to those in your industry, even to those who are outside of your membership. Perhaps the content will be useful as a compare and contrast or benchmarking exercise to a similar industry. Every opportunity should be looked at to widen the net, without of course diluting the content on offer to your core membership.

Chapter 2 - The difference between the member service ethos and the commercial ethos

Question: Is there an opportunity for you to earn event income outside your membership or from those stakeholders not so closely linked to your organisation?

Explaining the difference to other parts of the organisation

Events managers in member service who are moving towards a more commercial positioning sometimes have to defend the changes they have made; maybe it's been a rise in the price of a conference, which may appear high to someone, or the streamlining of a process, which means a little more work for members. The response to any criticism that events managers are reducing the quality of service or making too much money should be the same: *"You can't make money without running a good series of events which you are delivering to members who have the choice to attend."*

Another useful explanation events managers can use is that, at the end of this commercialisation, a lot less money will go to competitors and more money will flow back into their own organisation. And of course, that money can be used by the organisation on behalf of its members however it chooses.

Don't stretch too far!

When operating a commercial events department you have to remember not to stray too far from your natural territory. So don't go covering topics outside of your natural arena; targeting the non members who are exceptionally difficult to attract or running events that just don't fit with your objectives. And remember you should not deviate from the principles that underpin your current events strategy as we outlined in chapter one.

Chapter 3
Are events always the right option?

A lot of organisations can get hung up on events. They are an easy stand to hang a hat on. But events are not always the panacea they appear to be. So much comes down to the way your organisation and team is structured, staffed and skilled.

Before your organisation undertakes an event or series of events it should be asking itself if running an event is in fact, the best way to reach your objectives. Over the years organisations change but still they seem to run the same events in the same way. Sometimes the objective of the event has changed, but no one has told the event manager.

The main objectives of your events department are unlikely to change and are likely to be twofold:

1. To provide a structured and well delivered value added service to your members and stakeholders while making a profit or covering the direct and indirect costs involved in organising the event; or by losing as little money as possible

2. To provide services at a much lower cost than commercial competitors, or at no cost at all

These are worthy objectives for your department but to make them meaningful we have to consider the objectives of your stakeholders and members, for example are they looking to learn/network/meet suppliers?

We need to look at what events you should be offering your stakeholders or members to allow them to achieve their individual or their organisational objectives. Once we have an understanding of the department and your members/stakeholders objectives it's down to you to decide if running an event is the best way to meet all of these objectives.

Chapter 3 - Are events always the right option?

With your department objectives giving you some context and an understanding of your customers' objectives you should now move onto clarifying the objectives of each individual event. Some events will have very similar objectives, others will be very different. What is the end goal? What are you trying to do? What issues are you looking to cover? How much profit is desired? How many people are expected? From which part of the membership are they to come from? Once all these objectives are clear we ask the final question: How best can we deliver these objectives?

Internal objectives

The answer to the question: *"How best can we deliver those objectives?"* should be decided by your events team. What our organisations have to do is to concentrate the minds of the stakeholders or the staff in the organisation on the overall objectives. This refocusing will allow the events team to concentrate on how best to deliver those objectives. This is simply putting the objectives before the event and not the other way around.

In a commercially focussed events department which is objective led, many conversations still start with, *"We need to run an event on…"*, but after a good discussion around the department, the customer and the organisational objectives, the conversation ends up with, *"OK, that all makes sense, we won't achieve any of the objectives running an event, we'll do x instead"*. Conversations between a senior stakeholder and a well briefed objective led event manager will lead to events not being run if they are unlikely to reach their objectives. Now this is of course a big step for an event manager, saying no to a senior stakeholder, and this is why the event professionals in your commercial department have to be empowered.

If the organisation is clear about their objectives then a good events manager will know if an event can, or cannot deliver those objectives. In order to give senior management an idea when events should be used we have to look at what events are good for.

What events are good for

Events are very useful for getting a message out to a lot of people, who you know, will be interested in hearing that message, and will engage with your organisation. But in so many organisations familiarity results in the event being the first port of call, the default position when anyone wants to get a message out, engage their membership or earn income. But it's not always the best way.

Here is a list of possible objectives that an organisation may have. Underneath the objective is the type of event which the organisation could organise:

1. provide technical support on upcoming must know issues;
   half day seminars
2. provide a networking environment for members;
   evening forums with drinks
3. raise profile;
   series of well publicised events
4. develop a regional focus;
   series of regional seminars
5. address more general 'blue sky' issues in the sector;
   high profile annual conference
6. attract additional members
   overarching high profile conference

As you can see, events are very flexible and can tick many boxes. Without some context, this series of events looks like a great idea and you can just see the organisation diving into deliver a lot of events. And why shouldn't they; we've indicated that events can indeed deliver technical material and can of course be run regionally. More strategic events can look at the blue sky issues at a senior level, raising the profile of the organisation and with that profile attracting members from outside the membership. Don't we all just love events; they are the Swiss Army Penknife of the communications world.

But unless we look at the demand, the cost of these events and the alternatives, we don't have a true understanding of the validity of running events for all of these objectives. This is a step that a lot of organisations sometimes forget.

Chapter 3 - Are events always the right option?

Alternatives to events

Before we look at demand and costs let's think about other delivery options which an organisation may be able to use. This time we'll list the objectives and answer them without a pre-conceived idea that events are always the answer:

1. provide technical support on upcoming must know issues;
   detailed publication or an online publication on the specific area written by experienced industry professionals
2. provide a networking environment for members;
   evening forums with drinks
3. raise profile;
   allow the use of the SIG logo on industry trade magazines or link with a well placed sponsorship
4. develop a regional focus;
   regional newsletters
5. address more general 'blue sky' issues in the sector;
   electronic consultation on the general areas
6. attract additional members;
   advertise and raise awareness of the group nationally

Of course your organisation would have to look at this in its own particular way. One organisation may well be able to deliver a regional newsletter very easily and effectively. Another organisation that has to employ and train new staff, and engage the membership in a whole new line of delivery, will decide that this method is not viable.

Depending of course on the experience and resource of people in a particular department the organisation may not be able to tackle the objectives in all of these ways, but it does illustrate the point that objectives can sometimes be better achieved through other means and that objective led discussions often lead to quite different tactical deployment.

For Government agencies and departments and the larger charity, membership organisations and trade associations, the 12 options listed - that is, the six events in the first list and the mix of delivery options in the second - can almost invariably be delivered.

So next time you are tempted to say, *"let's run an event on..."*, just think if that is in fact the best way to start a discussion when considering how best to tackle an important issue.

Demand and costs

Each organisation's members or stakeholders may be more open to certain forms of delivery and that would affect the method of communication. But you started with the members objectives in mind, so you should have a good understanding if there will be a demand for the delivery. And of course the cost of delivering these services would have to be considered before a decision on which channels to use were made.

The demand from members and the cost of delivery should be important factors in deciding how to deliver these objectives and the role events should play in that delivery should be decided on that basis not on any whimsical idea that events are always the key.

In a commercial department costs are very important. Before we look at where we can save costs when delivering events we have to look at the other areas where senior management can make a positive impact on costs and allocation of resources: the other aspects involved in the event process that may lie beyond the influence of your event manager. This is the section where senior managers can delivery substantial value by focussing on the processes within the wider organisation that affect the day to day role of your events team and ultimately the delivery of your events.

Chapter 4

Addressing processes within the organisation

There are areas within the events process that may not be carried out by the events team, for example, this may be invoicing, programme development, administration or handling delegate bookings. If these processes are not managed with the same commercial eye that overlooks the event logistics and event management they are unlikely to be commercially lean and are likely to negatively affect the 'customer experience'.

The real bottlenecks in the event management process will come from the involvement of a Committee. As the American writer Elbert Hubbard said: *"a Committee is a thing which takes a week to do what a good man can do in an hour"*, and never is this truer than in our not for profit organisations.

Although part of the process of organising an event, the mechanics of managing volunteers involved in helping your organisation deliver services to members, has to be fully understood by senior management. If managers are trying to oversee the transformation from a 'member service' ethos to a 'commercial department', nowhere else is the understanding and support from senior managers more crucial than when dealing with this member/ volunteer part of the event process.

Managing your Committees

An active and engaged Committee can help enormously in the event process if handled properly, however, the involvement of a Committee or a volunteer panel in an event can also not only slow the process down but can seriously damage the event. It's a tricky balance.

A Committee's involvement should be limited to a pure advisory role. In some organisations Committees ask to see budgets; want to set prices; try to decide on duration; dates and the location of events. Sometimes I wonder why the organisation has a specialist events team in place if these decisions are allowed to be made by a Committee? However intelligent and experienced the professionals

Chapter 4 - Addressing processes within the organisation

on it may be, the Committee invariably lacks a single person with any event experience or event management qualifications.

Politics and the cultural make up of an organisation will determine the role that Committees have in your events and the wider commercial area. In most not for profit organisations they have a role to play in the event process, and as a senior manager you must have a say on how much they can manipulate the process. The organisation's commercial eye has to look at every process, including the role of a Committee.

An alternative to the reliance on Committees for content is to develop a close relationship between the events team and a member within a policy type role. In this environment the events team are creating and managing events themselves but work closely with the 'in-house' expert. This relationship tends to be easier to manage and the planning of the event normally moves much quicker, and has a greater chance of achieving more of the objectives than the organisations in which a Committees or volunteers have an unruly element of control.

Here are three examples of how commercial products can be damaged when a Committee has been let loose:

1. Too many sessions

A large Committee from a cross section of the industry was overseeing one of the organisation's largest events. As part of the justification for each member's place on the Committee, they considered it their duty to add a session to the conference programme. The motivation for these sessions was not to fill a well researched need for potential delegates but for Committee members to be seen to "add value" to an already bloated conference programme.

An excessive number of sessions led to a significant increase in costs and a decrease in revenue, as well as an over-complication for the event management.

2. Events can end up when and where a Committee wants it, not where delegates want it, or where it's cost effective to deliver it!

Managing a packed 90+ annual event schedule at one organisation was complicated enough. But when the events team had to schedule the event when

Chapter 4 - Addressing processes within the organisation

they would be sure they could manage it; when there were no big competitor events; in a place where they could find a suitable venue; that the delegates wouldn't mind travelling to; at a time of the year when delegates would be able to attend, and on a date where they could secure the keynote address, they also had to schedule this particular event around the diary of the chair. He wasn't speaking or chairing, he just "had to be there". Most of the delegates wouldn't have known him from Adam, and the selection of venue was over-complicated by his diary, and his personal 'decision', that anywhere north of Watford was a barren wasteland. As if choosing venues and dates wasn't difficult enough.

3. Relying too heavily on the Committee's knowledge

An online learning package was mooted by one organisation after research suggested that an increase in a specific area would demand extensive training and events wouldn't be the best way to deliver on the objectives.

From conception to completion of this e-learning product, with heavy involvement from the Committee, in not only designing the content but writing the material, the project took almost three years. An independent consultant had scoped the project completion at no more than six months.

Expanding on this example gives us a mini guide on how not to involve a Committee in a commercial product.

a. The project lacked direction and was not based on any clear objectives. The product was designed to address a need for members, but the primarily objective was to raise income for the association, yet this had never been fully understood by the Committee.

b. The Committee had volunteered to help write sections of the course. Expecting a busy executive to spend a significant amount of their time on a commercial product owned by the not for profit organisation is in most instances, unrealistic. These professionals are likely to be unpaid and will be scheduling this work around their many other work and life priorities. There will be an inevitable delay in content, and in a well oiled process this is a very tight bottleneck.

c. The Committee, without doubt, were experts on this particular subject but their knowledge of content was assumed by the organisation to leak into knowledge of price, placement and identifying the customer: this is the role of the marketers in your organisation, not a Committee. In the end the product designed was sold as a whole package, when a modular approach would have been much better for customers. The product was topic structured rather than structured around job function, making it harder to sell. The product was neither fit for the operational area nor liked by the training department of members' businesses.

How Committees should work with the commercial department

- A Committee should be used to identify possible topic areas for the not for profit organisation to cover for its members

- A Committee should be used as a sounding board for the provisional content and delivery. The Committees should not expect to decide how best this content should be delivered. That is the role of the commercial team

- The volunteers will be the first point of call if content is needed, for example a speaking slot at a conference. But proceed with care if you require them to give a significant amount of time to the project

- The Committee will be used to check content and should be kept up to date on the project's progress

- The volunteers will play a vital role as a marketing tool for that product, as recommendations and referrals by the Committee members will have a lot of merit among members

If your events team is having trouble with Committees see if you can get those Committees to sign up to the outline above, it might be easier than you think. Sometimes, the organisation and even the events team, assume that the Committees want control, and in return the Committee assume that they are expected to have control. In both circumstances you may find that both the Committee and the organisation are happy with the role as outlined above.

Chapter 4 - Addressing processes within the organisation

Maybe they are operating this way simply because it's always been done this way. But with a commercial ethos running through the organisations we are able to look at processes differently and say: *"Well what if we did it this way?"*

How to engage with the other crucial areas of the organisation

In most organisations politics don't play a major part and there is no deliberate stymieing of the delivery of providing added value services to members or stakeholders. However sometimes things still don't go smoothly. A common mistake is when employees from outside the events department are expected to help but this expectation isn't a shared one. If their role in the event process (not organising the events, but supporting in some way) isn't a core function of their job it is understandable that this support won't be a priority.

Question: Do all the staff in your organisation that interact with the commercial part of the business have this reflected in their job function?

There is a role for events managers to play in this too. With the support of senior management they have to make it clear what an important role these individuals who sit outside play in the event process; they are a valuable link in the chain and they have to be made to realise that.

We can use the examples of the administrator outside of the events team who is dealing with bookings, or your policy officer turning around text for a marketing email. One way of making sure that everyone involved in the events process knows their part is to design a Critical Path Analysis (CPA) document. This document shouldn't be complicated and doesn't need to be drawn on any fancy project management software. A sample and simple CPA is included in the electronic appendix.

The CPA shows the whole event process. For a conference with an exhibition it would cover topic generation, sponsorship and exhibitor sales, marketing dates, venue booking dates, timelines for speaker confirmations, etc. When others see that they are a crucial part of a chain, it is a lot easier to get them involved in the process as a whole. Another tip with the CPA would be to get all the stakeholders to sign up to the document - literally to sign it. This again helps tie them to the process.

The events team may be doing everything in its power to make your commercial events department run smoothly, but the problems may lie elsewhere, and if they do, they will need your help to solve them. A good CPA identifies all the parts of the process within the organisation which play a role in the delivery of your events. It doesn't solely focus on the events team and this should help senior management see the wood not just the trees.

Setting financial targets

Your commercial events team will not only respond well to financial targets but will need them if they are to add significant value to your members. Later in the book we will cover some benchmarking that will allow you to set targets but it is worth saying here that setting realistic and challenging targets for your events department is an essential role of senior managers. These targets shouldn't be, *"more than last year"* or *"break even this year"*, but should be solid numerical targets.

Setting a financial target and explaining to other senior managers, and stakeholders the importance of your team in achieving those targets, will be one of the best ways to support them. It will allow them to operate commercially and to run better events.

While you are ensuring that the rest of the organisation is ready to support the events team, you can also be making sure that you have the correct events team in place. The next chapter will allow you to benchmark your events team.

Chapter 5
What an excellent events team looks like

For a not for profit organisation's events department to function well, it must be led by an organiser in the true sense of the word. You should expect the head of the team to have some involvement in the selling, marketing, logistics and programme development of the events.

Commercial companies rarely employ generalists; they just can't find them and they won't dedicate the time to develop them. Commercial conference companies are like Smithsonian workhouses: salespeople sell, marketers market and programme developers generate what becomes the stuffing inside the sausage, rolling off the production line. This very structured and very demanding approach to work doesn't sit well in the work environment in the not for profit sector. These organisations are also solely focussed on profit. This is not the environment for your not for profit organisation or your generalist events manager. That is why if you get the right person - a generalist events expert - to lead the department, they are likely to be able to do a very good job for you.

Events managers in a not for profit organisation have to be more than a money making machine, churning out events on any topic in search of a 'hit'. If your events manager wanted to do that, they would work in another sector. The best events managers want their events to mean something more than just money to the organisation they work for.

It's often the case that there are skills in an events team that if honed and used elsewhere in the organisation can prove to be very useful. So this is a rallying call for your events team to come out of their shells, and you as the manager or the leader of the organisation to encourage them to do that. Your organisation will be a winner in the long run. There are a lot of things that events managers can do to help make events achieve better results, even when the going gets tough. Events managers need to step up, speak out and help the organisations they work for.

If you are the head of your events department and you don't organise or strategically organise, you have to ask is this the job for you, are you adding value to the organisation? If you spend all your time reporting back to senior management and members and managing staff you are not operating in a commercially focussed department.

As a senior manager, if you are looking at the events department as a commercial operation and the head of your event teams just oversees external event organisers, then you really have to question if you have the right person for that job. More fundamentally you have to consider if your department is structured properly. The role of the events manager shouldn't be to oversee the organising of an event, it should be to organise them.

As an example, your event manager doesn't put up the stage set, but they hire the company who do. They brief them, they make sure they arrive before the event and that they come in on budget. And they should be doing this with all of the parts that make up an event: they should not be managing an external company who oversees the events process.

Question: Do your events managers get their hands dirty and manage the events you organise?

The best people to organise events are always the rounded events person, those with experience across every part of the process, or those willing to learn and get their hands dirty. And if you have one in place already, you are a long way to making your events department a success. If you don't, you are already on shaky ground.

Your teams understanding of the balance between profit and service

As outlined earlier, one of the underlying principles of not for profit events is that you can run great events and not make money, but you can't make money without running great events. You have to have someone who understands the balance between profit and member service running your events department. It's not really a place for someone chasing every single penny, but it's also not the environment for someone with no commercial awareness.

Chapter 5 - What an excellent events team looks like

Benchmarking figure - what should your events be contributing?

As a general rule, an exceptionally focussed team of 4 events professionals should be able to manager 60-80 events per year, and generate a revenue around £1.2m - £1.5m. They might use a bit of outsourced resource now and again, but really most of the organising can be done in-house.

A good medium sized trade association or membership body should be looking to generate this level of turnover and a profit of £600K-700K shouldn't be unrealistic. If you run all your events with an eye on costs you really should be putting this number of great events on for around £500K.

Question: How does your team compare to the above figures?

Question: If you are not close to this figure, is it the lack of support from the rest of the organisation that may be getting in the way?

Question: What can you do to help?

The make-up of your events team

Now there may be a whole list of bottlenecks, reasons and excuses for not attaining this level of income, and they may come from the events team or from other parts of the organisation, and this may be a goal rather than a reality at this point, but by the end of the book you'll know what practical actions you can take to help your organisation achieve these sorts of figures.

So in the William Thomson dream team, your captain has been described as above; he or she is a solid all round events person with a firm grasp of commercial realism and a passion for events, as well as an understanding of the wider role your organisation plays.

The rest of your team would comprise of two logistical organisers, bright and willing enough to engage with your senior members to develop content, smart enough to know who to book to speak or entertain your audience. They should understand the principles of marketing.

The final and vital member of the team is your administrator, whose excellent customer service provides support across all of your events.

Demarcation of roles

When I set up event departments I always suggest the implementation of a clear demarcation in roles. The line drawn is one between the delegates and every other part of the event process.

I want my event organisers to focus on everything involved in the event except, and this might at first sound strange, "contact" with the delegates/guests. Obviously everything they do is focused towards the end user, but in this process the "contact" element must be separate. For example, when the phone rings and it's a speaker or a venue, I want my organiser to prioritise that above any other call.

Now delegate contact, this is where the administrator comes into their own. They should prioritise delegate calls and communications and bookings. In my model the delegate booking process doesn't sit with your finance department, and ideally it shouldn't. When the phone rings and it's a delegate who's confused, or wants to book, it's the most important call your administrator will take all day. And almost as importantly, they are likely to be able to solve the problem.

A common fault is to give the organiser this mixed set of priorities and have them involved in delegate communication. So if this isn't the structure of your current department, think about it.

Question: Is it the right one from a process and customer service point of view for your team?

Good event organisers and good event administrators come in all shapes and sizes, so I won't try to describe the ideal person. But suffice to say the organisers have to be mini team managers and your admin person has to have an eye for detail and a great customer service focus.

So that's "the who" bit dealt with. Now let's look at what that little team of four should be doing in our model.

The role of the events team

Your events team should be taking your events right through the event process: from conception through development, to delivery and then analysis. They should be strategically positioning their events against competitors and at the right price point.

Chapter 5 - What an excellent events team looks like

You organisation should be running the most cost effective events in your particular sector. Your events team should be taking all payments, sending all the invoices, producing packs (if you still do them), menus, flyers and badges, dealing with all the logistics and being the first port of call for your speakers and entertainers. They should be playing a part in the marketing of your events and securing sponsors and possibly exhibitors (the latter two could be outsourced in this model). And you should be doing this 60 to 80 times a year. This might all seem a lot for your events team to cope with but event organisers in this sector are a bit special and they can handle it.

A strong argument can be made for Professional Conference Organisers (PCOs) when events reach a certain size and also if your large congresses are international but most of our not for profit organisations, if led by the right event manager, following a commercial ethos, backed by senior management and the organisation can handle the majority of their own events, including the flagship ones. If they are supported by the rest of the organisation.

If the majority of your events are policy or content focussed, then to have this level of success, it is likely that you'll have to wrestle away some control of the planning process, including a move away from 'call for papers' and place that programme control with a well versed policy person. In order to do this successfully your events team will have to know their sector well, sourcing speakers and noticing topics that are being covered elsewhere.

Placing your commercial events manager in a senior enough position to do this will help achieve those figures and just imagine what your organisation could do with another £500K, how long could you maintain subscriptions at their current level, if this was coming in every year? Senior management must show confidence in their events team and they must empower them; the rewards are clear.

As long as you have the right processes and support, you and your team will be successful.

Part 2

How to make your events more commercial

Chapter 6
Nine steps to fantastic events

With the support and understanding of senior management and the volunteers in your organisation what's stopping you organising fantastic events? Could it be something as fundamental as your events team being unsure how to actually organise an event? Entering events departments to find experienced organisers managing events in quite a shoddy, unstructured and haphazard fashion does unfortunately happen.

Taking unnecessary risks by not checking if an event will go ahead before committing costs can be a common mistake. In other instances, departments don't market their events at the right time and even in one case a department creating the budget after the event had finished! We would hate all the support from senior management to be wasted if the actual event fell down. As it's the job of this book to help you make the most out of your organisation's events, it is worth checking that your events team are using a safe, tried and tested process.

Adopting the right event management process

This should be how every event is organised, almost without exception. This tried and tested method has been used to successfully manage rock festivals, dinners, training workshops and all manner of events. Depending on the size of each event, the time and importance of each step is magnified, but it is worth stressing that every event you are running or planning to run has to go through this process. If your event team's processes don't match this process, there is a good chance that, at a minimum unnecessary risks are being taken, and an outside chance that the events are being mismanaged.

1. Set measurable objectives

We will cover in detail the importance of objectives in the next chapter. We will therefore just summarise: make sure that an event is the best way to reach your objectives and that you can measure the success or otherwise.

Chapter 6 - Nine steps to fantastic events

The nine steps to fantastic events

1. Set measurable objectives
2. Draft budget/costs
3. Research market
4. Secure key factors first
5. Initially market event/ detailed research to tailor offering
6. Secure the remaining parts of the event
7. Get involved in the details
8. Run Event
9. Tie up the event

Chapter 6 - Nine steps to fantastic events

2. Draft budget / costs

There are a few tools which you will use and refer to throughout the planning of an event and the most important tool should be your budget.

In some organisations it may not be your normal practice to be beholden to the budget; in others the budget control might be extremely important. As an example, when organising a fundraising concert the budgetary control is pre-eminent: the objective is to raise as much money for the charity as possible.

At an early stage of planning the event manager should already be able to start building the budget, to add a few costs and estimate the income. They should have a profit figure in mind so they can look at likely income and what they have to spend to reach that target.

When making decisions on any part of the event your first port of call should always be the budget. In the charity concert example above, the organisers would have loved a US megastar to open the concert, and they wanted Muhammad Ali to welcome guests, and they would have loved champagne for everyone; a quick look at the budget when they put this event together showed them that what was actually feasible, rather than what was desirable. Remember our objectives? *"To make as much money for the charity as possible"*. The budget is the meat on the bones of those objectives.

In the end it was British boy band *Damage* who opened the concert, former Liverpool and England football player John Barnes who welcome the VIPs, and it was fizzy wine for all. All these decision were guided by a constant reference to the budget. If you use the budget and set it at the start of an event you should always be in control.

Always use the budget to control your event and also use it to help you achieve your objectives. If the objectives you have been set don't realistically match the money you are likely to earn or what you need to spend, use the budget as concrete evidence to renegotiate your objectives or seek approval for more money.

3. Research the market

Research is important and in general the more research you do on an event the smaller risk you will be taking. Your organisation's approach to risk will be a major factor as to how much research you need to do for an event; as will your own view to the level of research you conduct. At one organisation a series of events, which were free to attend, but still had a high profit target, were introduced only after a very long and detailed research process had been completed. These events were very similar to other events run in an equivalent sector but the organisations cautious approach to risk meant they checked the sanctioning of the events for a year. A SWOT analysis (Strengths, Weaknesses, Opportunities and Threats) and formal market research had to be completed.

In another organisation a £250K expenditure event on a similar topic was sanctioned after simply reading a new phrase in a few trade journals and a casual chat with the organisation's relevant policy officer. In six months the organisation had organised what would become the largest conference on that topic in Europe. Sometimes in the world of events, if you are after large rewards you have to take large risks.

Research had to be carried out on both these examples, but the degree of research was different. The culture of the organisations often determines the approach to risk and so of course does the experience of your events team.

4. Secure key factors of the event (perhaps keynote speaker, artist, venue)

For most events there will usually be one factor that will go a long way to making the event a success. For a conference it may be the opening keynote address; for a concert, when the performer is in town; for a dinner, when the venue is available.

Maybe you always knew what that factor was, or perhaps you were smart and while you were doing your research you asked about the "key factor". However we got here, we know that the headline speaker always attracts delegates, so this year maybe the conference has to be opened by the Industry's pre-eminent economist, or the dinner has to be at the wonderful venue on the Thames that everyone has been raving about. Not surprisingly the key factor is likely to be one of the most expensive, so it makes sense to have the amount identified at an early stage.

Chapter 6 - Nine steps to fantastic events

5. Initially market event/detailed research to tailor offering

In many cases, after following the first four points, you are ready to take your event to market. Marketing the event is a separate but a very much related process of organising your event and it will be covered in detail in Chapter 9. It is all about marketing the event at the right time. As we will explain, with increasing levels of information more people are likely to attend, but as you have a very close relationship with your stakeholders, and hopefully strength on which to build, you can go to market early with only a few details. And people will book to attend.

This step is there to make sure you limit your risk and make your event a success. Initial marketing will allow you to test the event before fully committing to it and it will also allow that bit of time to make any changes if they are needed.

6. Secure the remaining important parts of the event

These remaining parts are the other important areas. For a concert it would be the audio equipment, the other acts, the staging. For a conference it's the other speakers, or the final marketing programme. The important point here is that there must be a hierarchy in the things you spend time on. It's very unlikely that the small details are the things that make the big differences to your event. If you don't have food at your dinner it will be noticed considerably more than the fact that the place cards were not written in gold italics.

The inexperienced organiser will not have the familiarity with events to look strategically at the overall event, so to make a difference it will be the little things they concentrate on. The small things are easy to change and as the inexperienced organiser you can point out these small changes to management to prove that they have made a difference. At this stage we should be concentrating on the bigger things, the really important things. Not the details.

7. Get involved in the details

This is where we do look at the small things, the place cards; tinkering with the table layouts; making sure all the speakers are briefed; making sure that the email communication goes out with all the right information.

8. Run event

This is of course a full chapter, or a full book, or a full career, so there is no way we can sum everything up. And the step is fairly obvious. This is the time you spend at the event, making sure all the hard work you've done comes to fruition.

9. Tie up the event

It's back to the budget again, it's looking at stage one (the objectives), measuring that success and using that learning to improve your other events. After every decent sized event you run you should be able to spot at least two things that can improve your next event. Ask your audience, your exhibitors, and most importantly your experienced event professionals what they thought of the event.

What else your events team should be using to manage the event

Each event your team is running should have three things:

- a signed off list of objectives or a larger more detailed plan
- a timeline
- a budget

In the online appendix (details at the back of the book) you will find an example of all three. Just like avoiding any of the nine steps, if any of these documents are missing, or are ignored throughout the planning process, there will be risks, and there will be mismanagement.

Now we have briefly looked at the event management process we can look in detail at that important first step: setting objectives. This is the necessary strategic straitjacket which allows all the logistical and practical steps of organising an event to be taken with a strong element of control.

Chapter 7
The importance of setting objectives for your events

Before you get stuck into improving your events department and its events, think hard about one thing: should you be running events at all? Now of course, this book is not trying to put events managers out of a job, but it is trying to make sure that the events department is focussing its attention on organising the right events.

We covered earlier what events are good at doing and what other options should be available to you to deliver your objectives. This chapter looks at how you can decide if you have the right objectives, and why it is so important that you actually set objectives. Objectives have to be the foundation on which your events are built.

What objectives to set

For every event you are planning the objective setting stage should start with these three questions:

Question 1: What will a successful event look like to your customers and your organisation?

Question 2: What are the objectives of each individual section of this event and the event overall?

Question 3: How will you be able to measure the success or otherwise of your event?

These are the 3 most important questions you can ask during the whole event process and it is amazing how many organisations never ask them of their events. We all know that a lot of events are dreamt up by organisations without an adequate amount of research or are annual events that have always taken place; and no one has ever stopped to ask these fundamental questions. In commercial events departments you should be asking these questions for every event.

Chapter 7 - The importance of setting objectives for your events

Owing to the position of the events manager being about delivery rather than strategy, these are fundamental questions may not be expected of the events manager. However we would argue that it is fundamentally important that the person in charge of executing the event knows the answers to these questions so our events managers have to take control of their events.

The questions should be asked by the events manager to those senior managers and Committee chairs who want events, regardless of how difficult those questions will be to pose. Asking the questions should never be avoided. Remember, it is all about what is best for your members or stakeholders, and you can't know what is best until you find the answers to those questions.

Example

An events manager had to project manage the biggest international event for a large organisation. The event included a dinner in one of Hong Kong's most expensive hotels, followed by a full day conference at the same venue the next day. To set the scene the events manager was asked to take on the project when a few things had already been decided; the venue had in fact been booked and minimum numbers guaranteed months before they took over.

Like a lot of organisations they had jumped in thinking that, *"Well, we don't have a plan as such, but at least we have a venue"*. When this is the process the event ends up fitting the venue and the dates rather than the other way around, a clear example of what happens when the nine steps are disregarded. Objectives have to be set before any decisions are made on the event. They were without objectives because the previous event manager had never been told, but as we stated above, more importantly: they had never asked the three important questions.

The only 'objective' that had been set was to, *"Run the event very much along the lines as last year"*. Every event manager working in the not for profit sector will be very familiar with this original brief; it's unfortunately very common. Rather than push ahead the event manager thought, "What exactly is required?", "What does this actually mean?" In order to find out, she asked the three questions.

When the events manager asked the questions, and then acted on the answers, the dynamics of the event changed completely. And funnily enough they didn't

Chapter 7 - The importance of setting objectives for your events

run the event *"very much along the lines as last year"*, they ran a much better event for members and for the organisation.

So, for the first question:

Question 1: What will a successful event look like to your customers and your organisation?

The answer: "The guests at the dinner will see that we are a serious organisation able to help professionals and Government in Hong Kong address the important financial problems they face. The conference will demonstrate that not only is the organisation aware of the problems, but it will give its guests and delegates the answers. The event must come in on budget."

Question 2: What are the objectives of each individual section of this event and the event overall?

"The dinner should be used to raise the profile of the organisation in Hong Kong. It should be a PR exercise. This is not a member service.

The conference should be targeted at our current and potential future members in Hong Kong, and should be evidence that the organisation can deliver useful content and learning outside of the UK. This is the paid for member service."

Question 3: How will you be able to measure the success or otherwise of your event?

"We will hire a PR agency to manage the press at our dinner and conference. They can then also tell us how much coverage we receive in the English and Chinese press. In 3 months we will see a 10% rise in members joining the organisation in Hong Kong. The event will come in on budget."

After receiving these answers from the relevant heads of department the event changed dramatically giving the project team a real focus with clear direction. The event still took place but with a few fundamental differences. The invitations for the dinner were now focused on non-members, previously they had been for members. A PR element was added, which offered the organisation some real and useful measurements of success, and all of this was included in a project plan. They had direction on who should speak, because they knew who they were

Chapter 7 - The importance of setting objectives for your events

targeting to attend, and which topics they should cover, because they knew that press coverage had to be generated.

Think about how difficult it would have been for anyone in your team to run an event that was of benefit to members; to decide what the event should actually be focusing on; and measure the success without asking these 3 questions? It seems obvious but all too often it doesn't happen. The event that year was a roaring success: loads of press, loads of happy members, new members flocking to join. All the objectives achieved.

The event was such a triumph that it didn't run the following year. That might not sound like a success, but by using tools to measure its success it became clear that running the event again was never going to justify the loss the event would make. The organisation's objectives were achieved by some high profile meetings with Government officials and financial organisations and a marketing campaign.

It is possible that you are putting a lot of effort into a dinner which isn't making much money or a conference based on outdated objectives (or worse, based on no objectives at all). Therefore you should look at all your events and see how many of them answer all three questions adequately, and if you aren't satisfied with the answers, really ask yourself and senior managers, is this event still worthwhile? Or can we run the event differently to achieve those objectives?

The objectives described in the above example are the types of objectives that event managers want to be working to. Senior managers want to be avoiding the "same as last year" type direction to their event manager. They also want to make sure that the parts of the business that commission the events really understand how much value events can add.

It is likely that the event manager will need some practice coaching these objectives out of the relevant stakeholder in the organisation but it will be worth it. With more challenging objectives understood, set and achieved, the profile of the event manager and their team within the organisation will rise.

Chapter 7 - The importance of setting objectives for your events

How objectives differ and how they can be used

Here we will meet our fictional trade association "COSTA".

The primary policy interests of their membership are separated distinctly, with each area overseen by a Committee. Let's call these groups Policy Interest Groups (PIGs).

The PIG committee is there to consider the needs of *their* particular members by giving guidance to the commercial department. So the PIG sets its objectives and the commercial department decides how best to meet them.

We can ask each PIG what their objectives are. COSTA has to oversee the Committee and the commercial team to make sure that excellent member support through a series of commercial products is delivered (as part of the organisation's objectives). But for each individual PIG the objectives may be different, to explain: Here's a list of some objectives, the same ones we met in Chapter 3 when we looked at what events are good at delivering:

Possible objectives for each PIG:

- provide technical support on upcoming must-know issues;
- provide a networking environment for members;
- raise profile;
- develop a regional focus;
- address more general 'blue sky' issues in the sector and
- attract additional members

Each PIG will choose some of these as their most important objectives. For larger ones it is growing a regional membership; for small PIGs, it will be digging a foothold in the industry.

Once the objectives have been identified it is down to the commercial department to decide if an event is the best way to achieve those objectives and if it is, how best those events should be delivered.

Following this objective-led process puts the horse in front of the cart. You decide to run an event only once you have decided that the event is the best vehicle for delivering the prescribed objectives. This stops Committees, or other non delivery focussed parts of the organisation, needlessly getting involved in the details of delivery. They decide on the important objectives and then step aside to allow the professionals to deliver.

A realistic scenario?

This is an ideal scenario, one where the commercial department is able to decide how best to deliver objectives set by the organisation. This is the position your organisation should be aiming for: if you do this you stand a good chance of your events reaching a level where they can earn a significant income. If this was a common process, more high quality events would be delivered on time and within budget and you would have more satisfied members or stakeholders.

As an event organiser you have to use objective setting as a way to allow you to manage the events that you are being asked to organise, rather than the other way round. You understand the power, and the weakness of events and you have to be in the position to be able and confident to say 'no' to some of the more wacky and ill thought through events that will cross your desk.

In many of the not for profit organisations we work in it is difficult to say no to senior management, but asking them to explain their objectives and then asking them to allow you to explain how those objectives can or cannot be achieved through events will really give you the control that you need. It will also demonstrate that the events team should be left to organise those events, with management safe in the knowledge that they have delivered clear objectives and ways to measure the success.

With clear objectives and a decision that some events will be organised, let us look at how we choose the right events to deliver to reach our objectives.

Chapter 8
How to choose the right events

So you have decided that events can help you reach some of your objectives. Like all products and services events should be targeted and well researched.

In some organisations there is a lack of strategic direction: it's not clear at whom each event should be targeted. Is it members? Non members? Senior managers? Middle management? Sector specific?

Who should your events target?

Your organisation may be after the policy influencers, the decision makers, but in today's difficult environment it's a strong commercial events strategy to try and have ties at every level of membership. This isn't just a way to earn extra money; it is positively central to the survival of your organisation. Events are a very good way of engaging with those parts or people that are harder to reach.

The Institute of Chartered Accountants in England and Wales (ICAEW) is a great example of an organisation making sure it provides added value services to all 132,000 members.

As one of the largest membership body in Europe, keeping all of your members happy is an exceptionally difficult challenge. Segmenting the membership is the key and the ICAEW is great at this. Their 'Faculties' cover technical accounting disciplines like Tax and Audit, their Special Interest Groups cover market specific roles, such as Farming and Healthcare.

In order to catch everyone else in their membership they have products and services aimed at Young Professionals, Women and an executive network targeting board pipeline and current Directors. They also have products and services targeted at both accountants employed in business and accountants in practises. They also offer international events in hubs where membership is significant enough to earn an income.

The ICAEW's detailed and targeted approach leads to a very high level of engagement with all of their membership. Membership bodies (especially those

Chapter 8 - How to choose the right events

linked to a professional qualification) do this much better than other not for profit organisations because members will hopefully have a much longer connection, hopefully a lifetime membership and members are likely to connect with the personal development as well as the professional development of their membership body. Even though they have an advantage in the length of the members' likely membership, all not for profit organisations can adopt the principle in this multi layered approach to developing commercial products for their stakeholders.

Question: Can you split your service to members/stakeholders in a similar way to the ICAEW?

Targeting every level of the organisation makes solid business sense. You should be making every effort to ensure you are earning as much as you can through value added services, from a market, which is more familiar and easier for you to access. This is much more straightforward than trying to penetrate someone else's market; you can look to do this once you are on a solid footing with your current market.

Which events are best for you?

Below is a list of the type of events that not for profit organisations commonly run. We have given some detail of what normally works well for each event format and some commercial best practice benchmarking. We have concentrated on learning events but have also looked at more social events like dinners and lunches.

Dinners and lunches

Programme/entertainment: ranging from a welcome address by your chairman to an all-singing, all-dancing extravaganza

Marketing: Email and other electronic marketing plus general marketing, including a good looking online invitation

Exhibition and sponsorship opportunities: No exhibitors, a main sponsor, drinks reception sponsor and perhaps one more sponsorship opportunity. Limit this to high-value, high-ticket exclusive sponsorship

Price: Mid to high range. Full tables sold first and then single places

Continued over

Chapter 8 - How to choose the right events

Dinners and lunches (continued)

Lead in time: Work very well as annual events, so market with as long a lead-in time as possible (tables should start to be sold 5 months out)

Food: A very important part of the event. Normally silver service, at least 3 courses and wine

Room layout: Tables of ten, with each table booking a place on the table plan

Target audience: 150-1000+

Duration: Afternoon (for lunch) evening (for dinners)

Charitable aspect: Proceeds towards a particular charity, or charity raffle, silent auction, prize draw etc.

Half day seminars

Programme: 3 to 5 speakers with very detailed presentations drilling into the detail of the topic

Marketing: Email and other electronic marketing plus information in your newsletter, links form pages on your website

Exhibition and sponsorship opportunities: Sponsorship opportunities normally only with a series of events, rather than a 'one off' technical seminar but if you can deliver value to a sponsor then this is an option

Price: Low range, perhaps £125-£275

Lead in time: Short lead in time, perhaps 12 weeks from initial decisions on content to event delivery as this allows a fast and detailed response to technical issues (work exceptionally well for consultation to industry regulation)

Lunch: Included, normally hot or cold standing fork buffet to maximise networking over a short period of time

Room layout: Classroom or theatre style

Target audience: 40-80

Duration: Half day (mornings or afternoon)

Chapter 8 - How to choose the right events

Evening presentation

Programme: 1 to 2 speakers for an informal or softer topic to present

Marketing: Email invitation with web marketing

Exhibition and sponsorship opportunities: Limited opportunities

Price: Very low range, perhaps £75-£125

Lead in time: Short lead in time, perhaps 12 weeks from initial decisions on content to event delivery

Refreshments: Flexible depending on costs being covered but should include drinks and dinner/drinks reception

Room layout: Theatre style

Target audience: 30-60

Duration: Evening

Annual conferences and Congresses

Programme: 8 to 16 speakers in plenary format. With breakout options

Marketing: Email and other electronic marketing, newsletter and individual paper flyer and mailing (where applicable)

Exhibition and sponsorship opportunities: Branding available, including speaker slots as well as exhibition (limited depending on number of attendees)

Price: Mid to high range, perhaps £295-£400 per day

Lead in time: 40 weeks from initial programme meeting to event delivery but planning certainly could be 52 weeks

Refreshments: Lunch, hot fork buffet, or bowl food if you have a larger exhibition served in the exhibition hall

Room layout: Classroom or cabaret style, stage set

Target audience: 80-300+

Duration: Full day (possibly 2 or 3 days)

Branding: Individual and creative marketing should be used where possible

Chapter 8 - How to choose the right events

Free to attend conferences

Programme: 7 to 9 speakers in plenary format with breakout sessions x 5

Marketing: Email and other electronic marketing. Advertise 8-10 weeks out

Exhibition and sponsorship opportunities: Speaker slots available as well as exhibition (between 6-10 exhibitors)

Price: Free to attend

Lead in time: 24 weeks from initial programme meeting to event delivery

Refreshments: Fork buffet, or bowl food lunch in exhibition hall

Room layout: Classroom or theatre style, stage set

Target audience: 100-200

Duration: Full day

Branding: Individual

Chapter 8 - How to choose the right events

What type of event most accurately targets a particular level within your membership?

Events have a maximum impact when they target different levels of your member's or stakeholder's organisation. This market segmentation diagram should help you analyse if your current or planned events are targeting the right people. Don't be afraid to change from a conference to a seminar or from a seminar to a dinner if it is more likely to achieve your objectives.

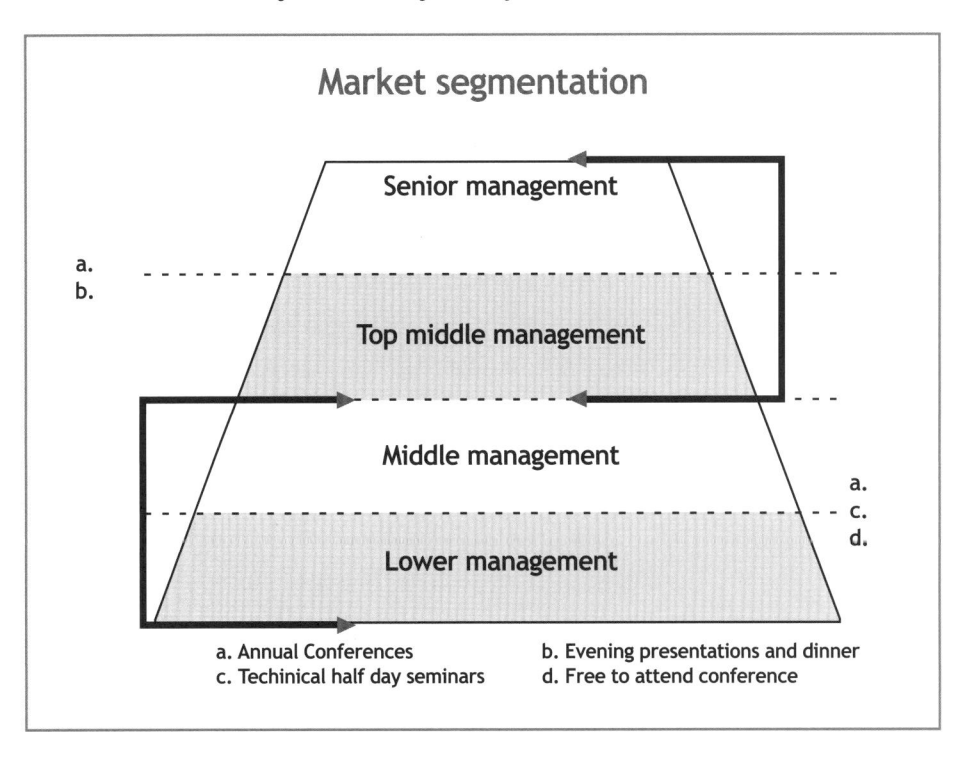

Market segmentation

Senior management

a.
b.

Top middle management

Middle management

a.
c.
d.

Lower management

a. Annual Conferences   b. Evening presentations and dinner
c. Techinical half day seminars   d. Free to attend conference

Some of the events you are running may not be the best way to engage the parts of your market that you are targeting. If you are looking to attract more technical level attendees, a one day conference may not be the best way: just because a conference has proven successful attracting a different level of your membership, it may not be the case for other levels.

Chapter 8 - How to choose the right events

Question: Can you look at your past and current event programme to see if you are offering different types of events to attract different level of seniority from your members or stakeholders?

It is likely - and if not it certainly should be considered - an objective of your organisation to be engaging not just on a political and policy level but also commercially with as much of your membership as you possibly can. Running events for every level of your membership, or groups of stakeholders, can work for your members and for your organisation, especially at renewal time when they are looking to measure the overall impact of membership.

Targeting non members

Using streams to attract non-members

One large trade association had been running a lot of events on one particular topic around regulation, which the industry had been dealing with for years. It had therefore been an area that the events department had focussed on for a long time and had run dozens of events covering the topic from all angles. It was therefore a very mature market and it was difficult to grow income from this stand alone topic. However, by chance, several new industries came under the same regulations.

The organisation had devised the industry guidance and found itself in a perfect position to offer this knowledge to other sectors. The organisation leapt at the opportunity and launched a conference directly targeting other sectors saying, *"learn from our industry, for years we've been dealing with the issues you are now facing"*. Over a two day conference the organisation ran two dedicated streams for those industries while looking at new developments in the area for their members. It certainly wasn't an easy sell for the events manager, as they had to access a market that wasn't natural to the organisation, but with some hard work the conference and a small exhibition grossed over £50K in the first year. Almost half of that came from outside the membership.

Run a conference with the majority of speakers from your organisation

It is very likely that as the experts in your sector you will be able to field some exceptionally knowledgeable speakers at a conference. You may also be able to undertake or commission specially targeted research that you can release at an event. This is your commercial intellectual property and you can use events to earn from it. Perhaps you can run an event dedicated to telling the wider world what you know, that they do not, or events detailing what others can learn about your members, or your sector. All these approaches can be very successful.

Awards dinners

Awards dinners are a very good way to earn a significant amount of income from outside of your membership. Offering awards to companies that supply products directly to your membership is an area that you (as an independent membership/community/Government organisation) are the natural and impartial organiser of, and have the edge on commercial conference companies and even trade journals that would usually host these kinds of events.

So with a clearly defined market targeted it's over to your event marketing to deliver those attendees.

Chapter 9
Events marketing strategy

Most not for profit organisations vie with large and small competitors from the commercial world but also to varying degrees against other not for profit organisation for many of their value added services. All of these organisations will be competing for your member or your stakeholder's hard earned pound. It is a very challenging environment to operate a business in but it's not uniquely competitive and it is not vastly different from the commercial world.

Despite the marketing exploits of commercial event businesses who have had a lot of success targeting your members, the not for profit sector as a whole has been slow to catch up and follow similar marketing strategies. The not for profit sector has lagged behind in moving from traditional styles of marketing and traditional delivery channels for their marketing. We have to ask why? In some organisations the problems can go beyond a suspicion of new marketing initiatives (as a cover for 'sales') to a disregard, or at least a downgrading of the discipline of marketing. If the power of marketing is not recognised or not given much weight or influence, this will be detrimental to your organisation.

Question: What importance do you place on the marketing function?

Marketers do sometimes bring this feeling of suspicion on themselves. Many a discussion between marketing managers or heads of marketing and managers from other departments often end with people feeling they have been bamboozled with complicated marketing theory and management speak. But marketing has some simple principles and with your events manager as the expert in the world of events they should have a serious input into the marketing activities for your events.

Marketing should work with your events department and this relationship would be better if your marketing department doesn't insist that marketing is some kind of dark art. This chapter should bring the two teams closer, as well as providing a quick guide to your event marketers and maybe even your marketing managers.

Chapter 9 - Events marketing strategy

Fundamentals of event marketing

Some not for profit organisations will be able to make significant improvements to their bottom line by simply addressing the way they talk about their events to their members and stakeholders. It is easy to move from 'information marketing', which is just telling people what's going on, to 'sales marketing', which is telling them what they are missing. Sales marketing is the marketing language of the outside world and most of your members/stakeholders will be accustomed to it, also and importantly it is being used against you by your competitors.

The natural progression of marketing in not for profit organisations:

Information Marketing -
"Tell them what's going on"

⬇

Sales Marketing -
"Tell them what they're missing"

⬇

Contextual Marketing -
"Tell them about it without them realising you are selling it to them"

⬇

Chapter 9 - Events marketing strategy

Picture your reluctant customer

The best way to move from information to sales marketing is to consider, even your engaged members or stakeholder, as a reluctant customer and this to be a vision shared by everyone involved in marketing. When picturing the 'reluctant customer' you think: *'What is it that will make that stressed and overworked manager step away from those day to day demands to pay to come to my event?'* You need to keep that image with you. If you follow this through all of your marketing, it almost singlehandedly changes your marketing. With this picture in mind you will find that marketing uses more persuasive (dare we say 'sales' language).

In your marketing you need to use words like "engage", "hear", "practical". Your reluctant customer doesn't have the time to be "involved". A lot of marketing in the not for profit sector assumes the delegate is as deeply engaged in the topic, as the organisation running the event. That's not always the case. Your reluctant customer needs to see words like "operational", "benefits" and "best practice" or he won't come, so tell him what he's missing. In tough market conditions, you would paint quite a different picture of your usual guest or delegate than in softer times, so in order to commercialise, your marketing has to reflect that.

Use 'sales marketing' to market your events

Here are a few fundamentals that your marketing must do if you are to compete against the other savvy not for profit organisations and the big commercial beasts, all of whom will be going after your members and stakeholders:

- Live in a competitive market: realise you have competition!
- Identify and use your unique selling points. You do have them
- Analyse your access to market. Don't use the same marketing channels for all your products
- Make information sticky. Perhaps drop in a useful chart or some stats on any paper mailings in order to try and get them to stay that bit longer on someone's desk
- Make information flow. Cross sell: it doesn't just make commercial sense; your stakeholders will see a joined up organisation too

Chapter 9 - Events marketing strategy

- Marketing communications and your message should be tailored to each group you are targeting; members; non members; associates and other stakeholders
- Realise that there is a difference in traditional (maybe just email) and non traditional channels (e.g. external website banner ads) and use where appropriate
- Realise that marketing is now a two way conversation and engage where possible and be open with delegates and guests
- Be open to the use of social media where appropriate
- Measure and identify success of each of your marketing campaigns
- Realise that the marketing 'mix' will be different for each style of product, and sometimes for each different product in that style
- Give the right level of information at the right time, to the right audience
- Separate a 'sales strategy' from a 'marketing strategy' where necessary. For lower priced products you can market; for more costly services and higher priced products, marketing will play a part in your more thorough and longer term sales strategy

Having identified the fundamentals that underpin your events marketing, let us look at the messaging.

What your events marketing has to say

The detail and order of your events marketing message is important and if used correctly can give you a big advantage on the competition. It is unlikely that another organisation will be in such a privileged position to cover the areas that you cover, owing to the amount of specialist resource and contacts that other parts of your organisation have, so you must use this to your advantage. This is the order of the messaging that would be sent to potential customers who know your organisation well.

When messaging to those potential customers who don't know you that well the first part of your marketing should be to 'prove your knowledge in this area/or even exactly who you are'.

Chapter 9 - Events marketing strategy

1. Put the content in perspective
2. Put the timing of the event in context
3. Excite and start to generate a compulsion to buy
4. Allow sufficient detail to generate bookings
5. Demonstrate your USP
6. List the benefits of attending

The words your potential customer likes to see

- Use words like; 'learn', 'engage', 'hear', 'understand';

- Use words like; 'practical', 'operational', 'current thinking', 'best practice', 'expert opinions and view', 'practical learning';

And always acknowledge the constraints on their time.

Contextual marketing

The first stage for any not for profit organisation when analysing their event marketing should be to identify what marketing style they have. As outlined earlier in this chapter if you are still 'member service' focussed, it is likely that the organisation will be sitting in the 'information marketing' position. If you are becoming more commercial you may have already moved to the 'sales marketing' phase. The final place for your marketing to land is 'contextual marketing'.

Contextual marketing builds upon the main strength of our organisations. It is likely that as the experts you are able to carry out or sanction paid-for research and you will be able to discuss and inform your stakeholders better than anyone on those particular topics. What contextual marketing allows us to do is to concentrate on messaging around 'hot topics', emphasising their importance to your stakeholders, while subtly mentioning the particular event you have arranged around the topic.

The correct use of contextual marketing is a fairly advanced stage for your marketing and it really has to be done subtly. If done correctly these contextual messages are very powerful. Contextual marketing works best as part of a longer sales process, when perhaps pitching something costly and time consuming, like in-house board training. It also works well mixed with sales marketing when attracting members who are not already engaged with your organisation.

The right amount of information at the right time
Example
A trade association with a well functioning commercial events department was able to open bookings for their scheduled events in 2011 by December 2010. There were over 60 events in total, stretching across every topic that the organisation covered. This trade association realised that there are many factors which determine when someone will be willing to buy/book a place at one of their events.

In the chart below, if we look at guest A, who has been coming to their annual dinner for years, the only information they will need is the date of the dinner and we can be sure that they will book way in advance. In terms of their buying decision, all other information for this guest is superfluous.

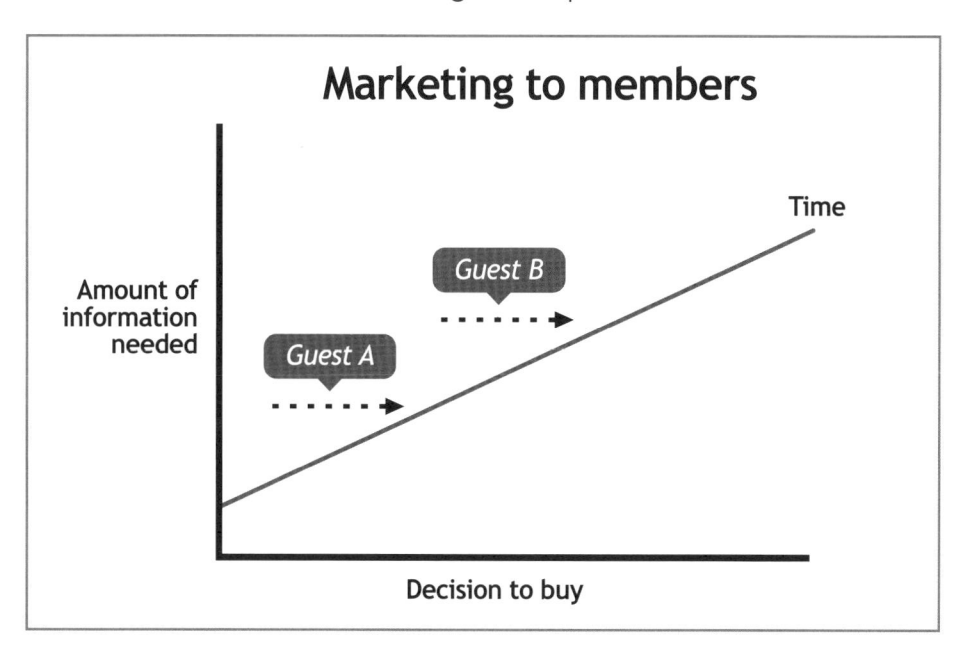

Marketing to members

Amount of information needed vs *Decision to buy* — Time increasing, with Guest A earlier and Guest B later along the decision timeline.

Chapter 9 - Events marketing strategy

For guest B, who's heard a few people talking about the annual dinner but has never been, she needs to know who the guest speaker is, what the venue is like and what else she will get for her money before making her decision to attend.

A lot of organisations don't market at an early stage. And we must ask - why not? Marketing as early as you can does two important things: it gives you an initial idea of the likely take up of the event before you've committed all your costs, and if it's a paid-for event, it gets some money in the bank.

As you are likely to have an established relationship with the majority of your members, the propensity for them to buy from you is hopefully quite steep; it is your target market after all! However when you are after non-members or the wider stakeholder community who don't normally buy from you, your marketing approach will have to be quite different and you would expect sales to flow once more detailed information was made available.

A lot of marketing material sent to those less engaged with the organisation tends to forget that the outside world might have other things on its mind.

If you do market to non-members and if you follow the detail and order of your marketing message as outlined in page 62, with a real emphasis on 'prove your knowledge in this area/or even exactly who you are', your marketing should hit its target. For people who don't know you, be humble. Tell those potential customers what your organisation is, who it represents and what it does, and most important, with a mixed use of sales and contextual marketing, why they should buy from you.

Chapter 10

Addressing the processes within the events team

Every events department is different. The way that your events department organises its events will differ completely from one organisation to the next. But with some analysis of your event management processes you will be able to streamline your service to members, stakeholders and anyone else who attends your events, and all this without negatively affecting the quality of your events. If you streamline your processes you will be able to concentrate on the most important areas of your event. And it's likely that you will be able to organise more events. And make more of a surplus.

When looking to review the processes in your events department and deciding what ones can be streamlined it is all about finding that balance between the organisational needs and organisational expectations; between the event team's knowledge and the influence of senior management.

Look to the event manager, not senior management, delegates or volunteers, when implementing change

In some organisations senior managers do not listen to the event experts, they listen only to the delegates, and worse than that, senior managers and volunteers sometimes assume that they know what the delegate or guest wants from their event. We really have to give the experts more of a voice.

If our organisations listen to their event experts it is very likely that there will be half a dozen or more ways that events can be delivered more cost effectively, more efficiently and with better results for your guests or delegates. It is unlikely that your delegates will be screaming for these improvements, or petitioning the organisations, and because the delegate isn't complaining, so the rationale goes, it means that things shouldn't change. Well that is seldom true: every event can be improved. If you look at every process with a critical economic eye,

Chapter 10 - Addressing the processes within the events team

improvements in your events will be a real possibility. If you wait for your delegates to point that out, it will be too late.

Events managers must take control of their events and implement the changes they think are necessary to keep up with the competition and to improve their events. Listed here are ten examples of processes that have been changed by events managers which have led to a better outcome for the delegates, as well as increasing, substantially, the efficiency of the events team.

As well as demonstrating some examples that your department can look to change straight away, one point worth emphasising is that none of these changes were demanded by delegates; they were noticed by experienced event experts, who were able to analyse the environment internally and externally and make changes to the processes in their departments. Attendees and even senior management don't have this vantage point, so take advantage of your events managers' view.

Common faults in event departments

1. Call for papers

A very antiquated call for papers process had been a monkey on the back of an events team within a membership body for years. It had been an initial battle for the events department to convince the organisation that the time had come to refuse hand written submissions and only accept typed copies. So it was a very brave move for the events manager to persuade the membership body to move to an electronic submission system in 2009.

With over 100 events a year, with the majority of programmes put together from call to paper submissions, the event organisers hadn't been focussing on what they do best: organising events, but rather had been caught up in a solidly technical and administrative task. Rather than place this task on to another department, or back to the volunteers, the forward thinking events manager investigated an electronic call for papers management system. The system was introduced and saved hundreds of work hours for the events team. Technology is not always the solution but sometimes it is.

Chapter 10 - Addressing the processes within the events team

2. Booking accommodation for delegates

A conference held in Brighton for over 500 elderly guests was a difficult one to organise for a team at one large trade association. A two day conference, with events for partners and a small exhibition, was unnecessarily complicated by senior management instructions to the events team to handle bedroom bookings for all the delegates. This was highlighted as an unnecessary burden by the event manager, but the answer was a standard not for profit one: *"That's how we've always done it"*. Well they had, and when they had 50 delegates it was manageable, but when the numbers increased it became a big distraction to the team. They stopped focusing on their core role of organising a great conference, or put a more familiar way, "On what they did best".

It took a flood in Brighton, 24hrs before the start of the conference, which took out 50% of the bedrooms, to act as the catalyst to change. As event staff struggled to take up the task of relocating delegates when they should have been overseeing the build up to the event, a rather soggy bunch of senior managers, who had been roped into help, were persuaded that a change in the process was needed.

The next year they used a centralised room booking agency. It was dedicated to that one task, run by accommodation professionals and not by the drowning harried event organisers. The service offered better rates for the delegates and it paid the trade association a small commission.

3. 90 sessions, 110 speakers over 2½ days!

I still have the brochure that advertised this conference and it is a treasure. It's the most complicated programme I have seen before or since. Just imagine almost one hundred sessions to choose from, and over one hundred speakers to see. More wasn't better: more was an over-complication for everyone involved. The programme lacked any kind of focus, had almost 50 speakers, who would have paid to attend the event and led to the most complicated schedule on the day for delegates, never mind the poor organiser.

The event had run for over ten years, and had seemed to grow in sessions to accommodate the growing numbers. But at some point, this surely becomes

Chapter 10 - Addressing the processes within the events team

unmanageable. After much debate and many distractions the number of sessions was reduced to just over sixty, with only eighty speakers: it was still a massive task. And after the changes, reducing ninety sessions to sixty sessions, there were still delegate comments relating to the content on the programme: "Too much choice", was a common response.

It is fairly common for large conferences to lose their focus. Every conference should have a theme. The number of sessions covered should relate to topics that need to be addressed: the programme shouldn't expand to fill a venue already booked, or expand to fit the number of days allocated to the event. The number of sessions shouldn't increase just because delegate numbers increase. More doesn't mean better.

4. Pre-booking sessions

Now that most of the events world has embraced online booking, this job is less demanding but some organisations are still blindly devoted to pre-booking sessions. If you need to pre book, why don't you do it on the day of the conference rather than before? When this is done, you wouldn't believe it, but there is no mad delegate panic, no stampede, and no complaints from delegates. Some cutting edge conferences are even letting delegates choose which sessions should run on the day, never mind which ones they should attend.

If you are still pre-booking sessions before delegates arrive without any back up from event technology, I strongly suggest you stop now.

The event mentioned in point 3, the one with the eighty sessions, believe it or not, had previously pre-booked every session. There was on average four streams running at the same time, with twenty sessions across the two and a half days. And there were over 800 delegates. So before they moved from pre-booking they had several event organisers inputting all these choices, some 6,000 inputs into a system.

And all this to avoid people turning up on the day and changing their mind. But what happened on the day, when this time consuming process had taken place back at the office? People saw their ex-work colleague was in another session, so changed; some delegates had booked so long ago that their job function had changed and wanted to go to another session. For a host of other reasons, the whole pre-booking process was a pointless and Herculean effort.

At one pre-booked event I saw an organiser tell a delegate that he couldn't go into a particular session because he hadn't booked. There was space, but it didn't matter as delegates who had booked might turn up and not get in. Of course they didn't, they'd changed their mind too. How crazy is this? Your delegate should be able to choose whatever he wants to do whenever he wants to do it. Pre-booking takes up so much time and really is, especially if you have someone close to the programme to judge which will be the most popular sessions, a waste of time.

Be brave. Trust your delegates. And trust your event organisers and your programme developers.

5. Guest handbooks for dinners

Unless you can earn more from advertising than what it costs to manufacture handbooks, you really should question why you would do these. If you don't have them, very few guests miss them. But one thing guests don't like doing without is a list of who is at what table. So using the venue's plasma screens, or printing some A2 posters spread around the room normally solves that. Or how about listing all the delegates on your website the day before and allow guests to print off the tables they are interested in?

Without the handbook you miss all the hassle of chasing delegates for their names for the book more than two weeks before the dinner. Live without the handbook, unless you can make money from it.

6. Delegate packs

Delegate packs used to be the most marvellous of things: hard covers, plastic slip folders, colour coordinated dividers, thick card inserts, as heavy as a brick, and as useful as a note pad and paper.

Thankfully with the green revolution to fall back on it is easy to dispense with this image and deliver everything online. A pack nowadays doesn't really have to have more than a programme, delegate list, and note paper.

Chapter 10 - Addressing the processes within the events team

So if you have your staff spending loads of time collating packs, collecting info for them, and spending hundreds of pounds on them, ask them why?

One organisation had a very bulky pack, full of presentations and flyers but they decided to change it overnight. They delivered all the presentations by email and only had a programme and notepad printed on the day. Over 1000 delegates attended this series of regional events. To test the success of this online presentation delivery format and minimum style pack on the day the team asked for feedback, with a positive response of 92%. The organisation thought they knew what was best and had insisted that packs were a must, but they weren't, the event organisers took hold, made the decision to change and was backed up by delegates. The delegates know what they wanted and the event organisers were able to deliver that in the most cost effective, efficient way. In other organisations the satisfaction with online packs has been even higher.

And on top of the delegate response, just think of the time, effort and money they saved not having to print and transport 1000 bulky delegate packs. And picture the delegates concentrating on the presenter and their presentation on screen instead of head down, reading through the presentation. As any learning expert will tell you, this is much more conducive to learning.

And whatever you do, do not try and replace packs with CDs or memory sticks. Doing so is much more hassle that it's worth.

7. Online administration

For a gala dinner of over 1000 guests the entire registration process was moved online. Previously it had been a part time role for one member of staff.

For around £1000 the system allowed guests to book a table, selecting it from a live floor plan, entering their delegate names and dietary requirements and amending their details at any time they wished.

The resource that was freed up from this event and four other similar events allowed the organisation to manage several five figure grossing events. It's amazing what these cheap and easy to use online event management systems can do. So try one.

8. Online payment

Some of your members will always want to pay by cheque or bank transfer and be invoiced, and if you currently do that, don't stop. But you should be offering the opportunity to pay online. Reduce the need to manually generate so many invoices, receive income up front and allow your guests or delegates to make that impulse purchase.

9. Pay attention to the event software you already have

When I worked with one organisation one of my first tasks was to find a replacement for the current event management system as it wasn't flexible and wasn't fit for purpose. So the first thing I did was test it. And would you believe, it was flexible and fit for purpose! It's just that no one had taken the time to understand it.

I was able to make some very quick system improvements by just using properly what was already there. Unfortunately the event industry is affected by technology flu as much as any other industry. So if you have a system, test it. Play with it. Ask another organiser to come in and rate it. I bet there is a good chance that it can do quite a few things that you didn't think it could.

10. Market with only a bit of information

A common process in some not for profit organisations is to "make a splash" and only market when all the details of the dinner are confirmed, or all the speakers are booked for the conference. As soon as you know the date and have a venue on provisional hold, why not advertise the event? And with a bit of planning most of your following year's events can be marketed well in advance.

You will have such a strong relationship with your members that people will buy from you with very little information. Take advantage of that, what's more, they will appreciate having as much notice as possible to avoid the hassle of having to move things around to accommodate the event later. And please note, this isn't a 'date for your diary' email it is an opportunity to book; and the later is much more efficient.

The final process within your events team, and the one that will make the biggest difference to your bottom line, is the process of cost reduction. And that's the subject of the next chapter.

Chapter 11

Why you always have to concentrate on costs

Perhaps you are surprised that we haven't looked at costs until Chapter 11. This is deliberate. Being commercial doesn't mean slashing costs indiscriminately. However, focussing on what your events department spends to achieve the surplus it does, should be an underlying principle with every one of your organisers in the events departments within not for profit organisations.

Your staff should be able to find the balance between offering members a good service and paying the right amount for products and services. They should be able to deliver these events while making the organisation money, or losing as little as is necessary. Cost should underpin every decision that your events team makes. Concentrate on costs and negotiate as much as you can. When suppliers are having as bad a time as you, ask and you shall receive.

Not for Profit Organisations - the soft target

In the past, and it's been our own fault, most suppliers would expect to receive a better rate for their services and products from our sector than the commercial world. And in the main it has been true. A lot of our organisations do tend to pay the higher end of prices for products and services and this is because they don't pay staff commission on bottom line or have a strong culture of cost cutting.

The first thing we can say to commercial organisations who want to increase the level of business they do with the not for profit sector is that our organisations are no longer soft targets for profiteering companies. A significant number of commercial companies are now targeting associations and institutes and now is the ideal time to play hard ball.

Example

In one not for profit organisation they were paying £50,000 over two years for an online system that handled bookings for a conference. It also did a few fancy

Chapter 11 - Why you always have to concentrate on costs

things like allow delegates to book and refuse meeting requests from other delegates. But basically it was an online booking system. The contract had been signed for the same annual event for two years and was worth £25,000 per year.

The offending (and offensive) supplier in question knew that the client was paying a vastly inflated price for the service but, as it was a not for profit organisation, they assumed that as long as they provided a good service, the charge would never be questioned.

As soon as the new events manager saw the details of the contract, they asked the supplier to come and discuss the second year of the contract. Expecting an informal chat around his bumper second year payout, he was taken aback when he was asked to explain the service in detail and cost each section of it. He waffled for a while. He was then told that the experienced events manager had costed his service with a company they had used before at £5K per event. He had overcharged the organisation at least £40,000 and he knew it, and he knew that the events expert knew it too. He wasn't surprised to see the contract not carried forward for the second year. This shows you the opinion that some suppliers hold, that service matters, and cost doesn't.

Question: *Do you have a number of supplier contracts that have never been renegotiated since your signed them? If so, why not get them in to discuss their service and ask to renegotiate any terms?*

Look at costs as much as you can. Managers should start the ball rolling by looking at current suppliers and questioning every contract. Hopefully you'll find that you negotiated a good deal in the first place but if not, you will be setting a marker for the rest of your staff that costs really are important. If your staff gets the message, your suppliers will too.

Good suppliers make their profit by providing a value for money service that will secure a long term relationship. We all have to emphasise that we are no longer a soft touch. If suppliers go for the short term gain after assessing that the current 'member service' ethos allows them to earn a huge margin, sooner or later, that organisation will move to a 'commercial department' and they will be first for the cull. By collective action on costs these companies will take heed. It's down to us to make sure we don't pay over the odds.

Chapter 11 – Why you always have to concentrate on costs

Only add what adds value

When you are looking for that competitive advantage it is easy to get carried away with potential new services and products and try to add something new to your events to provide some benefits to members. It is especially easy to do this for events that have run for a few years. Such motives shouldn't be discouraged of course but before you add the latest online appointment booking service or presentations on DVDs, you should have two questions: do they really add to the guest's experience and are they really value for money?

Think about the event from your customers' point of view. What do they really want to get out of the experience? The important things will be around what helps the delegates learn, engage with the event, with each other and of course enjoy the event.

Be strong and don't be persuaded by vanity purchases from your senior management who want to keep up with similar events they have been to. One financial services exhibition had its own exhibition TV station, despite the exhibition only having 40 odd exhibitors. If any guest noticed the station they certainly wouldn't have thought it added anything to their experience. However they may just have thought it was their trade association wasting their fees.

Network as much as possible

Networking with other event professionals is important not only for your organisation but your own personal development, so try and build contacts with other events managers. If you are running a not for profit organisation encourage your event manager to go to industry events and network with other event colleagues. Networks such as the Buyers Network Club, MemberWise, The Trade Association Forum and Association Resource offer excellent opportunities for this type of information-gathering networking. And associations like Meeting Professionals International are good ways to increase your skills and knowledge. Make the most of these meetings and find out what other organisations are paying for similar services and products.

Chapter 11 - Why you always have to concentrate on costs

Look closely at one of your biggest costs: venues

The largest and probably the most common contract you will sign is for the venue you use for your event, so you should pay this area more attention than most. Owing to the frequency you book venues and the cost it is therefore worth looking at venues in a bit of detail. Some of the principles we will cover can of course be related to any negotiation, but with a focus on something we all understand, you can save your organisation money and at the same time show the private sector that we can negotiate as hard as anyone!

If you are using a venue a few times this year and you have not negotiated a special rate, do so. And if you manage to get a good rate, ask them to backdate that rate. You might just be surprised at the response. This works and you can often receive credit notes for a couple or a few thousand pounds for events that you have already run. You really can cut almost every cost without reducing the quality of your events if you just ask for what you think is fair.

Even if you have found the ideal venue, think long and hard before actually signing a contract. Can you keep it on first option and hold off a bit longer? Could you say location "London" on your marketing material instead of naming the particular venue (this is very common in the commercial conferences world but less so with dinners, as the venue tends to be one of the most important parts of the event). If you are following the Nine Steps To Fantastic Events this will allow you to check the expected numbers before you confirm. A cost focussed team is the best risk mitigation you can have. Holding off confirming on a venue as long as you can will reduce your risk and increase the chance to make the money you need or to lose as little as you need to.

You should also look to book low minimum numbers, and make sure you negotiate a good decreasing rate for each delegate for any increase in the number of delegates who book. Venues are open to this and it is what their commercial customers do as a matter of course.

Minimum numbers

When choosing the right venue for your event it's important to get a good price for the hire. It's likely to be your largest single expense, so a small percentage

Chapter 11 - Why you always have to concentrate on costs

saving here can allow you to move some money to other areas of the event or on to your bottom line. The secret is to secure as reasonable a guaranteed minimum number of delegates as possible to secure the room you want. When you book the room you should also bear in mind a bit of scope for an increase in numbers.

The initial cost either for the hire or for a day delegate rate (DDR) is of course negotiable. But at this stage don't be persuaded to increase your minimum number for a smaller DDR rate unless you are positive you will get the numbers agreed. A lot of conferences waste thousands of pounds after being tempted by an increase in numbers for a lower rate, so why not just go back and negotiate once you actually have the numbers?

Sliding scale

The simple point to remember is that the more people you bring to a venue, the lower the delegate rate you can negotiate. Most venues will or should operate a sliding scale for business booked on a DDR. However some venues don't like to negotiate on these rates because, obviously, the higher the rate, the more money they make. But almost everything is negotiable and if you stay strong, you will secure a commitment to a sliding scale.

A word of caution. People who say they always get the lowest rates for things are the people who get the poorest service at venues. If you screw them down too much, they will cut back on staff, T+Cs and lunch. It's about finding the balance. Venue booking agencies are normally quite good at this, as they have to keep both parts of the equation happy, while of course making their cut. But with a knowledgeable team and a crack negotiator, the information in this chapter gives you good ammunition to reduce your costs.

In the world of events it is fair to say that everything is negotiable. Most of the organisations you deal with will quote top price first to everyone they work with. The public and private view of our industry, outside the clear 'charity sector', and this is especially true of the government sector, is that we'll pay whatever they ask. This is because we don't care about other people's money and we aren't particularly good at our jobs. Well that's not the commercial events mantra.

Chapter 11 - Why you always have to concentrate on costs

There are loads of good books and training workshops on negotiating skills and we don't want to try and cram this into a chapter but we have covered some things to think about when committing to your largest likely cost.

So if it is costs that impact your bottom line significantly they do to the same degree as your income. And it's pricing that we will therefore address next.

Chapter 12
How to decide on the right price for your events

In economic theory the price of a product is set where the company can maximise profit. They do this by generating as high an income as possible, while keeping expenditure as low as they can, and all this takes place in an environment where competitors are doing the same thing. This market activity will normally drive the price down or up to a level where organisations can make an acceptable profit, and economic theory states that people will pay that price.

This wasn't written for the world of not for profit organisations and in our sector it's never going to be as clear cut as this. Because of the political issues in trade associations and membership bodies, whose members are already paying a fee for membership, and in other not for profit organisations where they are subsidised or paid for by stakeholders, pricing is a little bit more difficult and tends to be a very thorny issue.

If we follow the principle that you have to run as cost effective an event as possible, and that you have an objective - to make some profit, to contribute to your organisation's bottom line - then charging the correct price will go a long way to meeting that objective. But when looking at events what is the correct price?

Free to attend doesn't mean no profit

'Free to attend' events can work extremely well for your organisation, allowing you to earn income from sponsors and exhibitors while letting members or your stakeholders attend for free and appeasing the 'member service' camp in the organisation. Series of free to attend events, normally one day conferences, are common now in a few different industries: IT, Finance and Banking.

Free to attend events are often used to attract the most senior of members. These people don't expect to have to pay to go to events, but as a commercial event organiser you still have to make money from such occasions. You must take

Chapter 12 How to decide on the right price for your events

advantage of the presence of so many leaders and decision makers by generating income from sponsors, who are of course, naturally keen to associate with the high level of attendee.

The commercial events industry in recent years has begun to focus on free to attend events targeted at the senior executive, paid for by sponsors in return for the exclusive access to those members. They are normally called Executive Networks or Executive Summits and some commercial organisations are making high six figure profits from these networks. Having a free to attend event doesn't necessarily mean a lower profit. Maybe it's no bad thing for the 'member camp' in your organisation to be pushing you to run events for free. Everyone's objectives can still be achieved. Executive networks can work well in the not for profit sector too.

Under £75. Be very weary when running events in this price range!
Example

One large membership body decided to run a series of regional events around a Government Green Paper discussing the future of their sector. The policy department were adamant that the organisation should run the events for free. At the time it was unlikely that the organisation would get any sponsor or exhibitors to sign up to cover the costs, so the commercial events manager was reluctant to run a series of events (eight had been suggested) because they would lose a significant amount of money.

The events had to come together in a very short period of time. Though it would have been easy to jump in and start organising, the events manager decided that even though timing was important that they shouldn't disregard the proper events process - 'The Nine Steps To Fantastic Events'. It took some time to get to the bottom of the objectives, uncovering in particular why the policy team had instructions to run the event for free. The answer to that question was that the policy team thought that 'free' would lead to the maximum possible attendance at these events. The event manager, being the expert, knew this was wrong, and spied a way of meeting all the policy team's objectives without losing money and could even look forward to a profit.

Chapter 12 - How to decide on the right price for your events

It's not easy to explain the universal law that approximately 30% of people don't show up for free to attend events and low priced events. Perhaps it's that attending for free reduces one's commitment to that event: investing money immediately makes you more likely to show up. There is also in many quarters a perception that a cheap event, will indeed be a 'cheap' event. In the end the organisation decided to charge a £75 fee. Later the organisation believed that they actually got more people to turn up (well certainly more than the policy team expected) on the day than they would have, had they charged nothing. It is of course impossible to know if more people would have turned up had the event cost less, but experience shows that more people would have certainly registered but certainly a lot more wouldn't have turned up on the day. Ultimately, hundreds of members attended the eight events, which made a small profit and both 'camps' within the organisation were happy.

You should avoid running events for less than £75. And you now have some solid arguments with which to fight your corner.

£75 - £195, your half day prices

Assuming that you have a reasonable profit margin as an objective, this is the range in which your dinners, lunches and half day events should be priced. Between £75 and £195 is the natural position that your events should occupy in the market. By keeping a tight grip on your costs, you should be able to make a good return. As you are targeting volume business, aim to charge somewhere between the two figures.

£200 - £395, your full day prices

Most one day conferences in the not for profit sector should sit squarely within this price range. This is considerably cheaper than similar conferences run by the commercial sector. Their business model, focusing on sponsorship as a major income source, allows them to make a very good margin with only forty or so delegates. Your business model has to be different. Remember your objectives: to provide a service to as many members as possible and to engage as many as possible.

A handful of conferences in our sector can charge that little bit more but, as a rule, this is the price band in which you should be operating.

Chapter 12 - How to decide on the right price for your events

What to charge members or your stakeholders compared to your non members

For member organisations the principle that should always be adopted is that the cheapest price to attend your events should always be for your members. You should not offer a rate to charities or government agencies that is cheaper than your member rate. Remember why you are here. You have a particular constituency and the price for them to attend your events should be cheaper than anyone else attending.

Although charging a certain rate can mean you miss out on the odd delegate or two from perhaps a charity that operates in your sector, there is a wider implication to be considered: offering the cheapest price to your members is a benefit to membership. Offering your member or stakeholders the cheapest price tells them that it's worth being a member. If you aren't a member you have to pay more.

Non-members should be charged at least £100 more than members for a full day conference. If you have an event that a lot of suppliers would wish to attend, don't be scared to charge £150 - £200 more. You have to weigh up the price of these suppliers attending as delegates in relation to the cost of an exhibition stand you may have at that event. You have to be careful that you aren't making your non-member attendance too cheap: you don't want these suppliers paying £1500 for four staff to attend and network instead of £3000 they would have to pay for a stand.

Is now the time to make a brave pricing decision - and brave can be both up as well as down?

Example

At one trade association their members were unhappy about the growing cost of their subscriptions. At the same time the association had noticed a decline in the number of attendees at their seminars and conferences. A drop off in subscription income as well as a drop off in additional revenue is of course not an uncommon position in today's environment. Increasing the subscription levels or targeting new members was not an option for the organisation, so to redress the overall

Chapter 12 - How to decide on the right price for your events

financial position of the organisations the events department were instructed to generate more revenue from events targeted at members.

The first decision the events department made was a very difficult one to justify to senior management in a falling market. They increased the cost of each half day seminar from £145 to £175. The organisation was very price conscious at this time and doubtful that they had any margin to increase revenue. If the pricing decision was wrong not only would revenue not increase, but it could potentially fall.

Of course, the event manager knew that simply increasing the price in such a market wouldn't have worked but they felt that if they concentrated on the quality of the programme, giving more details about each session in the initial mailing, they could show that the quality of their events was not commensurate with the current price, and thereby show that they had scope to raise prices.

The events team spent more time researching the topics, tidied up the programme content and made sure events had a longer lead-in time. Internally, the organisation felt more confident with a stronger product, and that in turn gave the events team more confidence when taking it to market.

More detail, given early to the delegates, filled them with a greater confidence to book their place. They proved to delegates that the association's events were worth attending and ultimately worth paying more for.

Thankfully, there was no decline at all in attendance. With over 40 seminars attracting on average 60 delegates, they were able to raise income by 15% (or over £70K) on these events alone.

In a difficult environment, a price drop isn't always the way to go. At the moment, some - maybe not all of your events, but some - will have a margin that will make a difference to your profit.

Question: If you look at your events is there one that just looks too cheap?

As one of the 4 Ps in the classic marketing environment (price, place, product and promotion), the price to attend is a key determinant of the success of your events.

The price you charge has to take into account the various internal aspects we have outlined that are peculiar to our types of organisations, but all too often not

Chapter 12 - How to decide on the right price for your events

for profit organisations don't price against the competition. This should always be given weight: what are other companies paying for access to your members? Although you would not be looking to change these prices, you should be aware of the external market value.

The commercial events manager should have the confidence to go up against events targeting their members/stakeholders which are run by commercial companies, knowing that what they do best in a lot of circumstances will be better than what their competitors do best.

Chapter 13
When and how to outsource parts of the events process

Like us as individuals, every organisation is good at doing some things and not so good at others. Too many not for profit organisations spend time doing the things they aren't particularly good at. Parts of the organisation may have once been good at certain things but that may no longer be the case. Others outside the organisation may well be in a better position to deliver these services or products to members or more crucially be able to help you deliver these services. Within the commercial events department rather than continuing to do things we are not best placed to do, we must look at outsourcing.

Strategic gap analysis

In most not for profit organisations the staff will be unsurpassed in their ability to put detailed content together for events like conferences, seminars and workshops. Staff from your organisation will be able to speak themselves or will be able to identify the right speakers. If you require external speakers, the power of your name will likely attract the people you want to speak. With all this fine content and great speakers, the events department will be able to market an event to a huge number of people (starting with your excellent membership database).

When looking to commercialise an events department one of the first things to do is find out what the current members of staff are skilled at. It's important to know initially where the resources of the department will be best focused to achieve results. In tough times like this your events department should be focussing on those things it does well; get back to your core business and what your members expect the events department to be doing and delivering.

Question: What do you currently outsource and why? If not why not?

What to outsource

What most not for profit organisations will not be so good at is spending time with companies who have only a loose connection to their market place, trying to understand the processes needed to secure those companies to sponsor or exhibit. There are very few true sales people prowling the corridors of our not for profit organisations; the characteristic they have are rarely mirrored in the culture of not for profit organisations and therefore don't quite fit. Selling is such a specialist skill that it is unlikely to sit within the make-up of a generalist events person. It is unlikely that our not for profit organisations miss having this skill in-house although every commercial organisation needs to embrace a degree of sales.

An efficient sales process (the distinction between sales and marketing is explained in earlier in chapter 9) is a priority for most not for profit organisations that need to raise additional income from outside of the membership. If you are targeting that income in the form of exhibition and sponsorship sales then you should be considering outsourcing this process. You should consider such a move, including outsourcing the administration of sales, covering any exhibitions stands at events, and then eventually look to outsource your sponsorship.

There is a strong argument for outsourcing sales because it allows your event manager and other staff to concentrate on building relationships with key suppliers, unencumbered by having to sell to clients.

The speed of the outsourcing process should be determined by the skills of the current staff and the experience of the organisation that will do your sales. If you have competent staff that can do an adequate job with sponsorship you don't need to rush to outsource everything. Staggering the process allows the company you have outsourced to time to get to grips with the industry, the contacts and, most importantly, you as a customer.

Why the not for profit customer is a difficult one

If you outsource you have to understand that your organisation will be a difficult one to deal with. Outsource to a company that understands the culture of your organisation and be sure to brief them very very well. Explain that your

Chapter 13 - When and how to outsource parts of the events process

organisation is not just after everyone's money (for example, the stands at exhibitions have to be relevant) and they have to feel comfortable saying 'no' to sales, and therefore missing out on commission if you the client, decides that it is best for your organisation to say no.

If you outsource your sales successfully you can have your team concentrate on organising the event (what they do best) and managing the relationship with the outsourced company.

Once the organisation has proved that they can sell within the particularly difficult environment you have set them, it is worth extending that process to look at your sponsorship sales.

There is of course an economy of scale in this. If all you are likely to ever sell is the odd stand here and there, your operation would be too small and too simple a process to outsource. But exhibitions are proven scalable businesses: where one exhibitor wants to get in front of your members, more will follow.

Sponsorship sales require a much better understanding of your organisation and your industry than the outsourcer needs to sell exhibition stands, yearbook advertising or website advertising. The relationship with sponsoring companies is much longer term, more strategic and needs more client management from your in-house staff. For example, a sponsor may want to make a welcome address at a dinner, or present a session at the conference they are sponsoring. These decisions have to be made by the internal events team, not by the outsourced company.

Other areas to outsource

As you no doubt know (because you are probably called at least once a month by venue booking agencies looking for business), one of the most common areas to outsource is help in securing venues. This is a very easy sell for outsourcing agencies because, as they will tell you, they are 'free' to use, they do all the hard work for you and they are the experts. This is all true, but it's not the whole truth. Did you know that these agencies earn 8% - 8.5% from the venue when they place business with them? Bear this in mind when they tell you they don't earn anything from you.

Chapter 13 - When and how to outsource parts of the events process

Event teams should use venue agencies if they are particularly busy; if they need to find venues in a city that none of the team is familiar with or if they are running a series of regional events. If you have a good negotiator in your team think long and hard about possibly paying 8-8.5% extra on your venue charge, as you are likely to be able to negotiate as good as the venue sourcing agency. If a venue really wants your business they have a margin that normally goes to the agency, which they can eat into to make you happy if they really want your business.

If there isn't a good negotiator in the team, if it isn't something that you do well, consider outsourcing. Remember the underlying principle of this and other chapters: concentrate on what you do well.

Justifying outsourcing to the rest of your organisation

Make the delegates/guests the most important part of your business. Argue that if your department, and therefore the delegate/guest/member/customer, can receive a better service elsewhere, you should outsource any of the processes that you use within the organisation. This could cover administration, delegate bookings (if you haven't moved online yet) invoicing and payments too, as well as the sales functions.

Example - lessons learnt from not outsourcing

For one organisation the event management process had undergone a major review and then a restructure. The event management process was working much better than before but not all the bottlenecks had been unblocked. The problems that the customers were encountering on their journey lay outside the responsibility of the events team, and unfortunately out of the event teams' control. The delegate bookings, invoicing and payments were performed centrally. No matter what the events team did they were unable to free the constraints from the customer journey.

The line manager who managed the invoicing department couldn't justify any extra staff member to deal with an increase in bookings because he didn't have the budget. His team couldn't cope with the demands and culture that expected delegates to receive confirmation of their booking within twenty four hours and

Chapter 13 - When and how to outsource parts of the events process

an invoice within the week. Unfortunately the events team were not allowed to look outside of the organisation to find a proper customer care service. In the end, the commercial business didn't work as well as it could have and the members weren't as happy as they should have been.

Example - lessons learned from outsourcing

In another organisation an outsourcing project didn't go at all well for the outsourcer or the company taking in the outsourced tasks. And from this experience were learnt five very important rules to outsourcing:

- Where possible consider outsourcing to an organisation that is around the same size as your organisation. If you are a large organisation, the company you are outsourcing to shouldn't be much larger than the department they will work for
- It is better to be a big fish in a small pond than a small fish in a big pond
- Do not outsource on price only. There are other important factors to consider
- Spend some time looking at the culture of that organisation and make sure it is similar to the culture of your organisation or at least your commercial department
- Outsourcing is a strategic move. Don't rush it

Once you have identified that outsourcing is needed, the secret to doing it successfully is to find good intermediaries who know their business, are willing to learn yours and who understand the unique culture of your organisation.

Conclusion

Not all not for profit organisations have to change the way they manage their events, nevertheless some do in order to compete in today's market. Many organisations need to change to survive. Trade associations and membership bodies need to modify to provide a better service to their members and Government bodies need to change to deliver events which are more cost effective.

Most people don't like change and we will probably all agree that most not for profits like change less than other types of organisations, this is normally for two reasons. One, there isn't a strong profit driver (and money does tend to sharpen the mind) and two, owing to the close relationship with their members or stakeholders, and that constituency being as averse to change as the organisation itself, change doesn't sit high up on anyone's agenda.

But we have to start to do things differently. A lot of trade associations and membership bodies used to be the unchallenged rulers in their particular specialist area, like British Rail or The Post Office, but now there is much more competition and with that, most not for profits have discovered the need to change.

Not for profit organisations are expected to be accountable and deliver as much value to members as possible, and to deliver those services as well and as efficiently as private enterprises. These are challenges that our sector is still coming to terms with.

This external scrutiny is forcing a lot of not for profits to look at the commercialisation of their operations. Membership surveys, feasibility studies, mapping of members, overall strategic reviews, a cost cutting culture, and even mergers are all likely to have been discussed within your organisation in recent times. Change is upon us and if we don't react to the new environment our organisations face at the very least a reduction in influence, staff cuts, and in extreme cases face extinction.

It is likely that the commercialising of your events may be on the horizon for a variety of reasons. As it's one of the most direct ways that your members or your

Conclusion

stakeholders interact with your organisation it has a prominent position; it may be one of your biggest potential revenue streams; possibly it's one of your large costs and is the next thing on your cost cutting agenda. Whatever the reason for commercialising your events you must make sure at the end of the process you still deliver an excellent service to members or stakeholders.

Next time you attend an event as a delegate and you come across a 'profit pariah', who asks; is profit that different from surplus? Or is profit really a four letter word? I hope the success you have implementing the ideas in this book means that he doesn't feel alone.

Bonus section

What's new in the world of not for profit events?

The one day profit driven, member only, free-to-attend conference

A new format doing the rounds within the commercial world that works much better in the not for profit environment is the "free to attend" conference. We mentioned this in the pricing chapter but I think it's worth looking at it in much more detail. You can introduce these events at your organisation with great success but as with any new event, it won't be totally plain sailing and you might have to overcome some early resistance.

This one day event is free to attend for your members (and it's important that it is a member only event). The programme has to be put together by an experienced programme developer with a good understanding of the topic or at least regular access to the in-house expert. It is a really hard programme to create.

The programme should contain a mix of sessions chosen by the programme developer. In addition, sessions hosted by companies paying for slots should be included in the programme, but of course it's not a free for all. Every session has to be relevant to some of the audience. Depending on the relevance of these paid for sessions, the subject is presented to the audience as a plenary if it will interest everyone; a sub plenary if it is likely to interest half the audience and a workshop if it is of interest to a smaller group of delegates. In order to make sure you are fair to the paying company, the cost of the session is related to the number of people to whom they speak.

As well as speaking slots, the companies buy a stand, and with it a good branding and sales opportunity. If you are likely to attract 80+ delegates, the cost should be approximately £7000-£10,000 for a plenary, £5000-£7000 for a sub plenary and £3000-£5000 for a workshop. With one plenary, two sub plenaries and four workshops you could earn £40,000 plus. Not bad for a 'free to attend event'.

The event is often something quite new, and that novelty can be quite scary. It's a handsome way to earn money for the organisation but there can be that horrible moment when management sees in its mind's eye 150 members being sold to for

Bonus section

30 of their valuable minutes by each exhibitor. *"What would the members say?"* they cry.

If you run an event where companies stand in front of your audience it's not like the old days when suppliers would just sell their products: most suppliers know that if they inform in sessions like this they are more likely to make a sale in the end.

The event has to lead with content. The conference programme has to stand up on its own merit. If it really is just several suppliers standing up and pitching, or softly pitching, it will bomb, but if you invite a few great industry speakers and structure some paid-for presentations around them, you really can put together a great programme that alone justifies the members' investment of time.

So, here's the list of benefits that I would try to get any doubting senior management to focus on:

- Free to attend for members. Members will like this!
- A member-only event: even if you want to come you can't, unless you are a member, which can be perceived as an added benefit of membership
- The programme will be content-led, with enough interesting and need to know topics for a full day programme
- As the event is free to attend you can quickly gauge if the event is going to attract the right number of delegates to make it viable. With a free to attend event you will get 50% of your likely attendance in the first week of opening bookings. The risk is limited because you quickly and easily gauge which members are interested
- If you choose your exhibitors well, the exhibition is actually seen as a good use of a member's time. You get two for one: a great conference and a targeted exhibition
- If you do it right, you make a lot of money. The earnings do not come from your members, but from the associated industry. You grow your commercial business without squeezing your members

There is an example programme in the electronic appendix, in case you've never been, or seen an event like this.

Online event delivery

Let's get straight to the key message, and the principal of online event delivery: **do not offer this service at a lower price than you charge your delegates to attend on the day**.

This is worth repeating: **do not offer this service at a lower price than you charge your delegates to attend on the day**.

The natural instinct within your organisation may well be to offer an online event at a discount on the basis that it is cheaper to deliver (you don't have to pay a day delegate rate for them, obviously) so why not pass this on to the delegate? A sound argument in the short run; but it's the long run we have to consider.

We won't debate here whether events delivered online are the future (there is contradictory research on this subject) but we can say with some security that some online delivery is very likely going to increase for learning events like seminars and conferences, but you won't find much interest in an online dinner.

So with the likelihood that at least some events will be delivered online, the last thing you should be doing is devaluing your events and charging a lower price; this is tantamount to strangling your future income. Why reduce the price and the profit margin? Why reduce the price for the content of this event and limit your earning in the future?

Example

One series of regional events, which took place in 2009, was on a pretty hot topic at the time, and had some far reaching impacts on the organisation's members. The events team ran 11 seminars around the country and charged members £125 to attend, which over 1100 people did.

After much discussion the event went on sale on line for £125, the same price as it cost to attend on the day. It was originally suggested to sell the online content at £75 as the events team surely had to offer the online version much cheaper the argument went. In the end, they sold 110 web seminars.

In order to increase the price from £75 to £125 the events team argued that they should sell the content for £125: they had five great speakers, delivering extremely

Bonus section

up to date and useful information to the members. They argued that, if you came to the event, you got lunch for free and you did some very useful networking, again for free.

If you watched at your convenience, decided not to spend any money on travel and have less time out the office, you missed out on the networking and lunch, but you got the content and a different set of extras.

If you message this correctly internally, focusing on the future earning and the value of your content, and then externally through some well written marketing, and set the right price in the first place for that content, you should be able to offer a valuable addition to your delivery of events without limiting the potential extra income this channel can offer.